THE COOK'S ENCYCLOPEDIA OF

ITALIAN COOKING

THE COOK'S ENCYCLOPEDIA OF
ITALIAN COOKING

CARLA CAPALBO

LORENZ BOOKS

This edition published by Lorenz Books
27 West 20th Street, New York, NY 10011

LORENZ BOOKS are available for bulk purchase
for sales promotion and for premium use. For
details, write or call the sales director,
Lorenz Books, 27 West 20th Street, New York,
NY 10011; (800) 354-9657

Lorenz Books is an imprint of
Anness Publishing Inc.

www.lorenzbooks.com

Publisher: Joanna Lorenz
Project Editor: Lindsay Porter
Designers: Patrick McLeavey and Jo Brewer
Photographer: Amanda Heywood
Prop Styling: Amanda Heywood, Carla Capalbo
Home Economist: Carla Capalbo
Assistant Home Economists: Marilyn Forbes,
Beverley Le Blanc, Wallace Heim

Previously published as *The Ultimate Italian Cookbook*

Printed and bound in China
Updated © 2001
10 9 8 7 6 5 4 3 2

CONTENTS

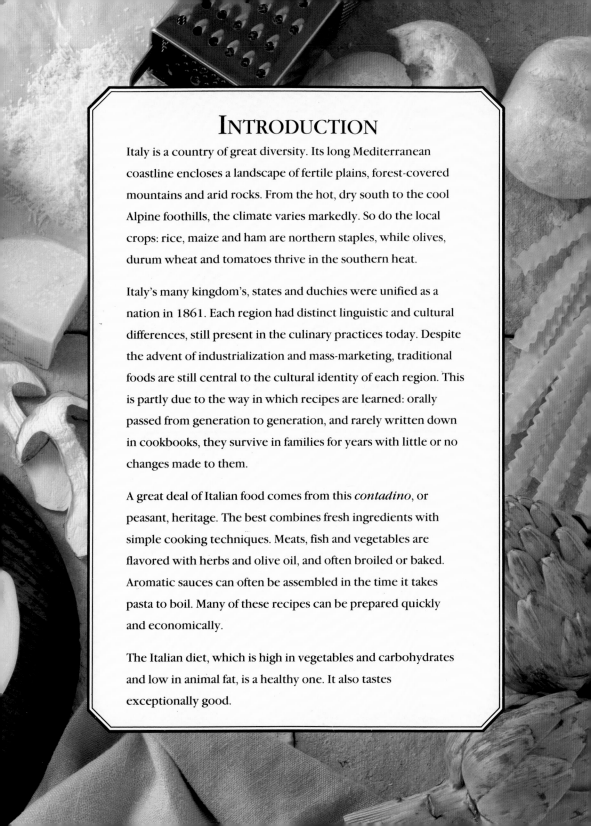

INTRODUCTION

Italy is a country of great diversity. Its long Mediterranean coastline encloses a landscape of fertile plains, forest-covered mountains and arid rocks. From the hot, dry south to the cool Alpine foothills, the climate varies markedly. So do the local crops: rice, maize and ham are northern staples, while olives, durum wheat and tomatoes thrive in the southern heat.

Italy's many kingdom's, states and duchies were unified as a nation in 1861. Each region had distinct linguistic and cultural differences, still present in the culinary practices today. Despite the advent of industrialization and mass-marketing, traditional foods are still central to the cultural identity of each region. This is partly due to the way in which recipes are learned: orally passed from generation to generation, and rarely written down in cookbooks, they survive in families for years with little or no changes made to them.

A great deal of Italian food comes from this *contadino*, or peasant, heritage. The best combines fresh ingredients with simple cooking techniques. Meats, fish and vegetables are flavored with herbs and olive oil, and often broiled or baked. Aromatic sauces can often be assembled in the time it takes pasta to boil. Many of these recipes can be prepared quickly and economically.

The Italian diet, which is high in vegetables and carbohydrates and low in animal fat, is a healthy one. It also tastes exceptionally good.

Fresh Produce

Italian cooking is based on the creative use of fresh, seasonal ingredients. Vegetables and herbs play central roles in almost every aspect of the menu. In the markets, there is a sense of anticipation at the beginning of each new season, heralded by the arrival, on the beautifully displayed stalls, or the year's first artichokes, olives, chestnuts or wild mushrooms. Seasonal recipes come to the fore and make the most of available produce.

Many of the vegetables once considered exotically Mediterranean are now readily available in the markets and supermarkets of most countries. Fennel and eggplant, peppers, zucchini and radicchio are now increasingly present in pasta sauces, soups and pizzas, as well as wonderful accents to meat and fish.

Wherever you shop, look for the freshest possible fruits and vegetables. Choose unblemished, firm, sun-ripened produce, preferably locally or organically grown. Fresh herbs like basil, parsley and sage are easy to cultivate in window boxes and gardens and have an infinitely finer flavor than their dried counterparts. Italian cuisine is not a complicated or sophisticated style of cooking, but your recipes will benefit immeasurably by starting with the best quality ingredients you can find.

Below: *Italian cuisine does not rely on unusual produce, but it must be as fresh as possible.*

Kitchen Cupboard Ingredients

Perhaps the single most important ingredient in a modern Italian kitchen is olive oil. The fruity flavor of a fine extra-virgin olive oil perfumes any dish it is used in, from pesto sauce to the simplest salad dressing. Buy the best olive oil you can afford: one bottle goes a long way and makes a huge difference to any recipe.

Balsamic vinegar has only recently become widely available outside of Italy. Made by the slow wood-aging process of wine vinegar, the finest varieties are deliciously mellow and fragrant. The taste is quite sweet and concentrated, so only a little is needed.

Porcini mushrooms are found in the woods in various parts of Europe in autumn. They can be eaten cooked fresh, or sliced thinly and dried in the sun or in special ovens. A few dried porcini soaked in water adds a deliciously woodsy flavor.

Olives are one of Italy's most wonderful native ingredients. Unfortunately, freshly cured olives do not travel very well, and many of the most delicious varieties are not available outside the Mediterranean. Sample canned or bottled olives before adding them to sauces as they sometimes acquire an unpleasant metallic taste that could spoil the flavor of the dish.

A typical Italian store cupboard also contains a supply of dried, natural ingredients. Dried beans, lentils and

Above: *An Italian kitchen might have a selection of dried beans, pulses and rice; olives, olive oil and good quality vinegar; as well as dried spices and other flavorings.*

grains are stored in air-tight dispensers for use in soups and stews. Polenta, the coarsely ground yellow maize, is a staple of the northern Italian diet, as is the rice used to make risotto. Of the special varieties grown in the area for this purpose, the best known are Arborio, Vialone Nano and Carnaroli.

Capers, pine nuts, sun-dried tomatoes, dried chilies, juniper berries and fennel seeds are some of the other ingredients commonly used to give Italian dishes their characteristic flavors, and are good basics to keep in the kitchen cupboard.

Meats and Cheeses

Antipasti do not always entail large amounts of preparation, and are often simply composed of the ingredients typical of the region. A popular antipasto consists of a plate of mixed prepared meats and sausages. Salamis, pancetta, air-dried bresaola, coppa and mortadella sausages are some of the meats most commonly used in Italy, often served with an accompaniment of crusty bread and butter. Prosciutto crudo, raw Parma ham, is the most prized of all meats, and is delicious served thinly sliced with ripe melon or fresh figs.

An Italian meal is more likely to end with a selection of cheeses and fruit than a sweet dessert. Among the huge variety of cheeses, the following are some of the best known:

Gorgonzola is made in Lombardy and is a creamy blue cheese. It has a mild flavor when young, which becomes stronger with maturity.

Mascarpone is a rich, triple-cream cheese with a mild flavor. It is often used in desserts as a substitute for whipped cream.

Mozzarella is a fresh, white cheese made from water buffalos, or, more commonly, cows milk. The texture is soft and chewy and the taste mild.

Parmesan is a long-aged, full-flavored cheese with a hard rind, used for both grating and eating in slivers. The large wheels are aged from 18–36 months.

Fresh Parmesan is superb, and is incomparably better than the ready-grated varieties sold pre-packaged.

Pecorino is made from ewes milk, and comes in two main types, Pecorino Romano and Pecorino Toscano. This salted, sharp-flavored cheese is widely used for dessert eating, and for grating when mature.

Scamorza is made from cows milk. Its distinctive shape is due to being hung from a string during aging.

Below: *A typical Italian meal might include cured meat as an antipasto, and finish with cheese instead of a sweet dessert.*

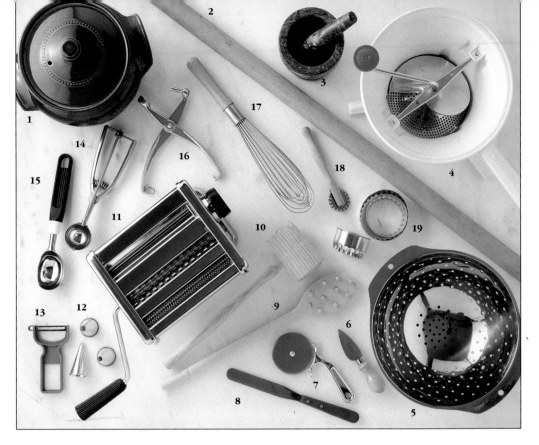

Equipment

1 *Earthenware pot*. Excellent for slow-cooking stews, soups or sauces. Can be used either in the oven or on top of the stove with a metal heat diffuser under it to discourage cracking. Many shapes and sizes are available. To season an earthenware pot before using it for the first time, immerse in cold water overnight. Remove from the water and rub the unglazed bottom with garlic. Fill with water and bring slowly to a boil. Discard the water. Repeat, changing the water, until the 'earth' taste disappears.

2 *Pasta rolling pin*. A length of doweling 2 in diameter can also be used. Smooth with sandpaper before using for the first time.

3 *Pestle and mortar*. For hand-grinding spices, pepper, herbs and breadcrumbs.

4 *Hand food mill*. Excellent for soups, sauces and tomato 'passata': the pulp passes through the holes leaving the seeds and skin behind.

5 *Colander*. Indispensable for draining hot pasta and vegetables.

6 *Parmesan cheese knife*. In Italy Parmesan is not cut with a conventional knife, but broken off the large cheese wheels using this kind of wedge. Insert the point and apply pressure.

7 *Pizza cutting wheel*. Useful for cutting slices, although a sharp knife may also be used.

8 *Spatula*. Very useful for spreading and smoothing.

9 *Spaghetti spoon*. The wooden 'teeth' catch the spaghetti strands as they boil.

10 *Meat hammer*. For pounding escalops. Also useful for crushing nuts and spices.

11 *Pasta machine*. Many are available, including electric and industrial models. Most have an adjustable roller width and thin and wide noodle cutters.

12 *Icing nozzles*. For piping decorations, garnishes, etc. Use with a nylon or paper pastry bag.

13 *Wide vegetable peeler*. Very easy to use for all sizes of vegetable.

14 *Italian gelato scoop*. Good for soft ices that are not too solid.

15 *Ice cream scoop*. Better for firm and well-frozen ice creams.

16 *Olive pitter*. Can also be used for pitting cherries.

17 *Whisk*. Excellent for smoothing sauces, beating egg whites.

18 *Fluted pastry cutter*. For cutting fresh pasta or pastry.

19 *Cookie cutter*. Also used for cutting fresh pasta shapes.

Pasta

Pasta in its many forms is a staple of Italian cuisine. These are just some of the varieties available.

1 *Alfabeto.* Small alphabet pasta for soups.

2 *Anellini.* Little rings used in soups and broth.

3 *Canneroni.* Pasta rings for thick vegetable soups.

4 *Capellini.* Very fine "angel hair" pasta, can be broken up and used in broths.

5 *Chifferi piccoli lisci.* Smooth, macaroni-like pasta used in baked dishes.

6 *Chifferi piccoli rigati.* Ridged version of the above.

7 *Conchigliette.* Small shells used in soups.

8 *Conchigliette rigati.* Small, ridged shells used in thick soups.

9 *Conchiglioni rigati.* Large, ridged shells used for stuffing and baking.

10 *Ditali.* Used in soups, traditionally with dried beans.

11 *Ditalini.* Soup pasta, smaller than ditali.

12 *Ditalini lisci.* Smooth ditalini, also used in soups.

13 *Elicoidali.* Good for baked dishes, or those with chunky sauces.

14 *Fagiolini.* "String beans" used in soups.

15 *Farfalle.* Butterflies or bows. Excellent with shrimp and peas and in cold pasta salads.

16 *Fusilli.* These spirals are ideal with tomato and vegetable sauces.

17 *Fusilli integrali.* Whole wheat spirals. Good hot or cold with thick vegetable sauces.

18 *Fusillata casareccia.* The twisted shape is good with tomato sauce.

19 *Gnocchi.* Shells for chunky vegetable or meat sauces. Gnocchi tricolori (19a) is flavored with tomato and spinach.

20 *Gnocchi integrali.* Whole wheat shells popular in vegetarian dishes, hot or cold.

21 *Gnocchetti sardi.* Sardinian shells. Good with lamb or fish sauces.

22 *Lasagne doppia riccia.* Frilly-edged lasagne. This is a dry version of the popular egg pasta, used for stuffed and baked dishes.

23 *Lasagne verdi.* Spinach gives this lasagne its green color.

24 *Lingue di passero, Bavette.* Traditionally paired with the classic pesto sauce.

25 *Linguine, Bavettine.* This finer version of lingue de passoro is good with fish sauces.

26 *Lumache rigate grandi.* These large, ridged "snails" are suitable for thick sauces with strong flavors such as olives and capers. Also good for pasta salads.

27 *Macaroni.* This is the English version of Italian maccherone, most popular baked with cheese.

28 *Mafaldine.* This is often eaten with sauces made from soft cheeses, such as ricotta.

29 *Mezze penne rigate tricolori.* The pasta is tinted with tomato and spinach to produce Italy's favorite colors.

30 *Orecchiette.* Dry version of the traditionally hand-made pasta popular in the south of Italy. Cooked with green vegetables.

31 *Penne lisce.* Quills or pens. Cut diagonally to catch more sauce.

32 *Penne rigate.* Ridged quills, a favorite shape in Italy. Great with tomato sauces.

33 *Pennoni rigati.* Large ridged quills. Good for baked dishes.

34 *Peperini.* Little pasta dots to add to broth or soups.

35 *Perciatellini.* This is a hollow spaghetti. Can be used with any of the usual spaghetti sauces.

36 *Pipe rigate.* "Ridged pipes". Good for thick, chunky sauces with peas or lentils.

37 *Puntalette.* For adding to soups and broths.

38 *Rigatoni.* Often baked with meat sauces and cheeses. Mezza rigatoni (38a) are smaller in size.

39 *Ruote.* Pasta wheels, always popular with children.

40 *Spaghetti integrali.* Whole wheat version of spaghetti (40a), more popular abroad than in Italy.

41 *Spaghettini.* Finer version of spaghetti, good with delicate sauces.

42 *Stelline.* Little stars, another small soup pasta.

43 *Tagliatelle.* Dried egg noodles, good with creamy sauces.

44 *Tagliatelle verdi.* Dried spinach-flavored egg noodles.

45 *Tomato spirals.* Specially made tomato-flavored pasta.

46 *Tortellini.* Small dumplings, often cooked and eaten in broth.

47 *Tortelloni.* Pasta dumplings stuffed with meats or cheeses.

48 *Zite.* A long hollow pasta often used with fish or tomato sauces.

2

28

48

35

24

25

40

40a

41

48

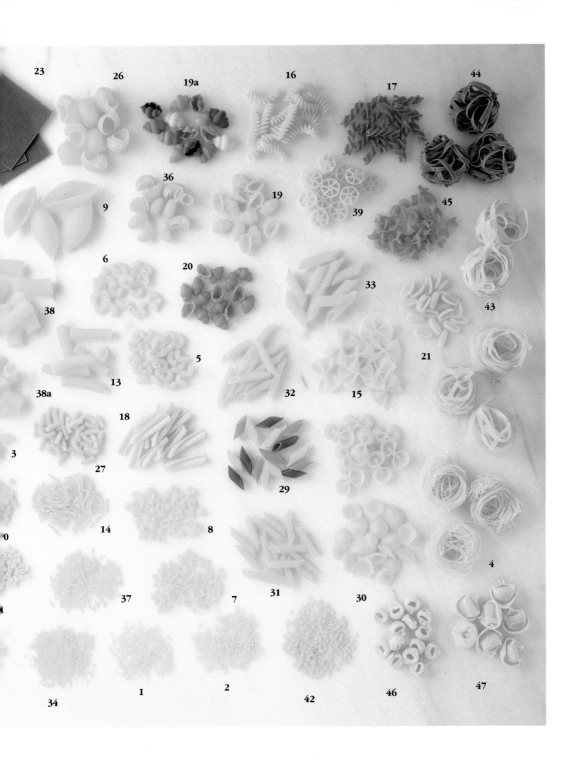

ANTIPASTI AND SOUPS

Hot or cold antipasti are the perfect start to any meal, and are also great for parties. Hearty vegetable soups with grains and pasta make warming first courses and nutritious light meals.

Raw Vegetables with Olive Oil Dip   *Pinzimonio*

Use a combination of any fresh seasonal vegetables for this colorful antipasto from Rome,
where the dip usually consists only of olive oil and salt. The vegetables should be raw or
lightly blanched, and the olive oil of the best quality available.

Ingredients
3 large carrots, peeled
2 fennel bulbs
6 tender stalks celery
1 pepper
12 radishes, trimmed of roots
2 large tomatoes, or 12 cherry tomatoes
8 scallions
12 small cauliflower florets
For the dip
½ cup extra-virgin olive oil
salt and freshly ground black pepper
3 tbsp fresh lemon juice (optional)
4 leaves fresh basil, torn into small pieces
(optional)
serves 6–8

1 Prepare the vegetables by slicing
the carrots, fennel, celery and pepper
into small sticks.

2 ▲ Cut the large tomatoes into
sections if using. Trim the roots and
dark green leaves from the scallions.
Arrange the vegetables on a large
platter, leaving a space in the center
for the dip.

3 ▲ Make the dip by pouring the olive
oil into a small bowl. Add salt and
pepper. Stir in the lemon juice and
basil, if using. Place the bowl in the
center of the vegetable platter.

Celery Stuffed with Gorgonzola   *Sedano ripieno di Gorgonzola*

These celery stalks are very easy to make. Serve them with drinks, or take them to a picnic.

Ingredients
12 crisp stalks celery, leaves left on
½ cup Gorgonzola cheese
½ cup cream cheese
fresh chives, to garnish
serves 4–6

1 ▲ Wash and dry the celery stalks,
and trim the root ends.

2 ▲ In a small bowl, mash the cheeses
together until smooth.

3 Fill the celery stalks with the cheese
mixture, using a spatula to smooth the
filling. Chill before serving. Garnish
with chopped chives.

Crostini with Cheese

Crostini con formaggio

Crostini are small pieces of toasted bread. They can be made with various toppings, and are served hot or cold with drinks. This cheese-topped version is always popular.

Ingredients
4–6 slices day-old white or brown bread
¾ cup thinly sliced cheese (fontina, Cheddar or gruyère)
anchovy fillets
strips of grilled red pepper
freshly ground black pepper
serves 6

1 ▲ Cut the bread into small shapes (triangle, circle, oval, etc.). Preheat the oven to 375°F.

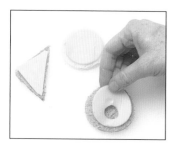

2 ▲ Place a thin slice of cheese on each piece of bread, cutting it to fit.

~ VARIATION ~

For a colorful addition use strips of green or yellow pepper.

3 ▲ Cut the anchovy fillets and strips of pepper into small decorative shapes and place on top of the cheese. Grind a little pepper on each.

4 ▲ Butter a cookie sheet. Place the crostini on it, and bake for 10 minutes, or until the cheese has melted. Serve straight from the oven, or allow to cool before serving.

Crostini with Mussels or Clams

Crostini con cozze o vongole

Each of these seafood crostini is topped with a mussel or clam, and then baked. This recipe comes from Genoa. Use fresh seafood whenever possible.

Ingredients
16 large mussels or clams, in their shells
4 large slices bread, 1 in thick
3 tbsp butter
2 tbsp chopped fresh parsley
1 shallot, very finely chopped
olive oil, for brushing
lemon sections, to serve
makes 16

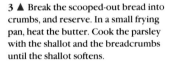

3 ▲ Break the scooped-out bread into crumbs, and reserve. In a small frying pan, heat the butter. Cook the parsley with the shallot and the breadcrumbs until the shallot softens.

4 ▲ Brush each piece of bread with olive oil. Place one mussel or clam in each hollow. Spoon a small amount of the parsley and shallot mixture onto each mollusc. Place on an oiled cookie sheet. Bake for 10 minutes. Serve at once, while still hot, with the lemon sections.

1 ▲ Wash the mussels or clams well in several changes of water. Cut the "beards" off the mussels. Place the shellfish in a saucepan with a cupful of water, and heat until the shells open. (Discard any that do not open.) As soon as they open, lift the molluscs out of the pan. Spoon out of their shells, and set aside. Preheat the oven to 375°F.

2 ▲ Cut the crusts off the bread. Cut each slice into quarters. Scoop out a hollow from the top of each piece large enough to hold a mussel or clam. Do not cut through to the bottom.

Mixed Seafood Salad

Insalata di frutti di mare

All along Italy's coasts versions of this salad appear. Use fresh seafood that is in season, or use a combination of fresh and frozen.

Ingredients

12 oz small squid
1 small onion, cut into quarters
1 bay leaf
7 oz shrimp, in their shells
1½ lb fresh mussels, in their
  shells
1 lb fresh small clams
¾ cup white wine
1 fennel bulb

For the dressing

5 tbsp extra-virgin olive oil
3 tbsp fresh lemon juice
1 clove garlic, finely chopped
salt and freshly ground black pepper

serves 6–8

1 ▲ Working near the sink, clean the squid by first peeling off the thin skin from the body section. Rinse well. Pull the head and tentacles away from the sac section. Some of the intestines will come away with the head. Remove and discard the translucent quill and any remaining insides from the sac. Sever the tentacles from the head. Discard the head and intestines. Remove the small hard beak from the base of the tentacles. Rinse the sac and tentacles well under cold running water. Drain.

2 Bring a large pan of water to a boil. Add the onion and bay leaf. Drop in the squid and cook for about 10 minutes, or until tender. Remove with a slotted spoon, and allow to cool before slicing into rings ½ in wide. Cut each tentacle section into 2 pieces. Set aside.

3 ▲ Drop the shrimp into the same boiling water, and cook until they turn pink, about 2 minutes. Remove with a slotted spoon. Peel and devein. (The cooking liquid may be strained and kept for soup.)

4 ▲ Cut off the "beards" from the mussels. Scrub and rinse the mussels and clams well in several changes of cold water. Place in a large saucepan with the wine. Cover, and steam until all the shells have opened. (Discard any that do not open.) Lift the clams and mussels out.

5 ▲ Remove all the clams from their shells with a small spoon. Place in a large serving bowl. Remove all but 8 of the mussels from their shells, and add them to the clams in the bowl. Leave the remaining mussels in their half shells, and set aside. Cut the green, ferny part of the fennel away from the bulb. Chop finely and set aside. Chop the bulb into bite-size pieces, and add it to the serving bowl with the squid and shrimp.

6 ▲ Make a dressing by combining the oil, lemon juice, garlic and chopped fennel green in a small bowl. Add salt and pepper to taste. Pour over the salad, and toss well. Decorate with the remaining mussels in the half shell. This salad may be served at room temperature or slightly chilled.

Prosciutto with Figs

Prosciutto crudo con fichi

The hams cured in the region of Parma are held to be the finest in Italy. Prosciutto makes an excellent starter sliced paper-thin and served with fresh figs or melon.

Ingredients
8 ripe green or black figs
12 paper-thin slices prosciutto crudo
crusty bread, to serve
unsalted butter, to serve
serves 4

1 ▲ Arrange the slices of prosciutto on a serving plate.

2 ▲ Wipe the figs with a damp cloth. Cut them almost into quarters but do not cut all the way through the base. If the skins are tender, they may be eaten along with the inner fruit. If you prefer, you may peel each quarter carefully by pulling the peel gently away from the pulp.

3 ▲ Arrange the figs on top of the prosciutto. Serve with bread and unsalted butter.

Cherry Tomatoes with Pesto

Pomodorini con pesto

These make a colorful and tasty appetizer to go with drinks, or as part of a buffet. Make the pesto when fresh basil is plentiful, and freeze it in batches.

Ingredients
1 lb cherry tomatoes (about 36)
For the pesto
1 cup fresh basil
3–4 cloves garlic
4 tbsp pine nuts
1 tsp salt, plus extra to taste
7 tbsp olive oil
3 tbsp freshly grated Parmesan
cheese
6 tbsp freshly grated pecorino
cheese
freshly ground black pepper
serves 8–10 as an appetizer

1 Wash the tomatoes. Slice off the top of each tomato, and carefully scoop out the seeds with a melon baller or small spoon.

2 ▲ Place the basil, garlic, pine nuts, salt and olive oil in a blender or food processor and process until smooth. Remove the contents to a bowl with a rubber spatula. If desired, the pesto may be frozen at this point, before the cheeses are added. To use when frozen, allow to thaw, then proceed to step 3.

3 Fold in the grated cheeses (use all Parmesan if pecorino is not available). Season with pepper, and more salt if necessary.

4 ▲ Use a small spoon to fill each tomato with a little pesto. This dish is at its best if chilled for about an hour before serving.

Hard-boiled Eggs with Tuna Sauce

Uova sode tonnate

The combination of eggs with a tasty tuna mayonnaise makes a nourishing first course that is quick and easy to prepare.

Ingredients

6 extra large eggs
1 × 7 oz can tuna in olive oil
3 anchovy fillets
1 tbsp capers, drained
2 tbsp fresh lemon juice
4 tbsp olive oil
salt and freshly ground black pepper

For the mayonnaise

1 egg yolk, at room temperature
1 tsp Dijon mustard
1 tsp white wine vinegar or fresh lemon juice
⅔ cup olive oil
capers and anchovy fillets, to garnish (optional)

serves 6

1 Boil the eggs for 12–14 minutes. Drain under cold water. Peel carefully and set aside.

4 ▲ Fold the tuna sauce into the mayonnaise. Season with black pepper, and extra salt if necessary. Refrigerate for at least 1 hour.

5 ▲ To serve, cut the eggs in half lengthwise. Arrange on a serving platter. Spoon on the sauce, and garnish with capers and anchovy fillets, if desired. Serve chilled.

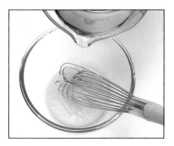

2 ▲ Make the mayonnaise by whisking the egg yolk, mustard and vinegar or lemon juice together in a small bowl. Whisk in the oil a few drops at a time until 3 or 4 tablespoons of oil have been incorporated. Pour in the remaining oil in a slow stream, whisking constantly.

3 Place the tuna with its oil, the anchovies, capers and lemon juice in the bowl of a blender or food processor. Process until smooth.

Tuna and Bean Salad

Tonno e fagioli

This substantial salad makes a good light meal, and can be very quickly assembled from canned ingredients.

Ingredients

2 × 14 oz cans cannellini or borlotti
    beans
2 × 7 oz cans tuna fish, drained
4 tbsp extra-virgin olive oil
2 tbsp fresh lemon juice
salt and freshly ground black pepper
1 tbsp chopped fresh parsley
3 scallions, thinly sliced
serves 4–6

1 ▲ Pour the beans into a large strainer and rinse under cold water. Drain well. Place in a serving dish.

2 ▲ Break the tuna into fairly large flakes and arrange over the beans.

3 ▲ In a small bowl make the dressing by combining the oil with the lemon juice. Season with salt and pepper, and stir in the parsley. Mix well. Pour over the beans and tuna.

4 ▲ Sprinkle with the scallions. Toss well before serving.

Carpaccio with Arugula

Carpaccio con rucola

Carpaccio is a fine dish of raw beef marinated in lemon juice and olive oil. It is traditionally served with flakes of fresh Parmesan cheese. Use very fresh meat of the best quality.

Ingredients
1 clove of garlic, peeled and cut in half
1½ lemons
¼ cup extra-virgin olive oil
salt and freshly ground black pepper
2 bunches arugula
4 very thin slices of beef top round
1 cup Parmesan cheese, thinly
    shaved
serves 4

1 Rub a small bowl all over with the cut side of the garlic. Squeeze the lemons into the bowl. Whisk in the olive oil. Season with salt and pepper. Allow the sauce to stand for at least 15 minutes before using.

2 ▲ Carefully wash the arugula and tear off any thick stalks. Spin or pat dry. Arrange the arugula around the edge of a serving platter, or divide on 4 individual plates.

3 ▲ Place the beef in the center of the platter, and pour on the sauce, spreading it evenly over the meat. Arrange the shaved Parmesan on top of the meat slices. Serve at once.

Tuna in Rolled Red Peppers

Peperoni rossi ripieni di tonno

This savory combination originated in southern Italy. Grilled peppers have a sweet, smoky taste that combines particularly well with fish.

Ingredients
3 large red peppers
1 × 7 oz can tuna fish, drained
2 tbsp fresh lemon juice
3 tbsp olive oil
6 green or black olives, pitted and
    chopped
2 tbsp chopped fresh parsley
1 clove garlic, finely chopped
1 medium stalk celery, very finely
    chopped
salt and freshly ground black pepper
serves 4–6

1 Place the peppers under a hot broiler, and turn occasionally until they are black and blistered on all sides. Remove from the heat and place in a paper bag.

2 ▲ Leave for 5 minutes, and then peel. Cut the peppers into quarters, and remove the stems and seeds.

3 Meanwhile, flake the tuna and combine with the lemon juice and oil. Stir in the remaining ingredients. Season with salt and pepper.

4 ▲ Lay the pepper segments out flat, skin side down. Divide the tuna mixture equally between them. Spread it out, pressing it into an even layer. Roll the peppers up. Place the pepper rolls in the refrigerator for at least 1 hour. Just before serving, cut each roll in half with a sharp knife.

Stuffed Mussels

Cozze gratinate

This tasty appetizer is a speciality of southern Italy. It can be made equally well using large clams. Always use the freshest seafood available.

Ingredients

1½ lb large fresh mussels in their shells
⅓ cup unsalted butter, at room temperature
¼ cup dry breadcrumbs
2 cloves garlic, finely chopped
3 tbsp chopped fresh parsley
¼ cup freshly grated Parmesan cheese
salt and freshly ground black pepper
serves 4

1 ▲ Scrub the mussels well under cold running water, cutting off the "beard" with a small knife. Preheat the oven to 450°F.

2 ▲ Place the mussels with a cupful of water in a large saucepan over moderate heat. As soon as they open, lift them out one by one. Remove and discard the empty half shells, leaving the mussels in the other half. (Discard any mussels that do not open.)

3 ▲ Combine all the remaining ingredients in a small bowl. Blend well. Place in a small saucepan and heat gently until the stuffing mixture begins to soften.

4 ▲ Arrange the mussel halves on a flat cookie sheet. Spoon a small amount of the stuffing over each mussel. Bake for about 7 minutes, or until lightly browned. Serve hot or at room temperature.

Egg and Cheese Soup

Stracciatella

In this classic Roman soup, eggs and cheese are beaten into hot broth, producing a slightly 'stringy' texture characteristic of the dish.

Ingredients
3 eggs
3 tbsp fine semolina
6 tbsp freshly grated Parmesan cheese
pinch of nutmeg
6¼ cups fresh or canned beef or chicken stock
salt and freshly ground black pepper
12 rounds of French bread, to serve
serves 6

3 ▲ When the stock is hot, and a few minutes before you are ready to serve the soup, whisk the egg mixture into the broth. Raise the heat slightly, and bring it barely to a boil. Season with salt and pepper. Cook for 3–4 minutes. As the egg cooks, the soup will not be completely smooth.

4 ▲ To serve, toast the rounds of French bread and place 2 in the bottom of each soup plate. Ladle on the hot soup, and serve immediately.

1 ▲ Beat the eggs in a bowl with the semolina and the cheese. Add the nutmeg. Beat in 1 cupful of the cool stock.

2 ▲ Meanwhile heat the remaining stock to simmering point in a large saucepan.

Minestrone with Pesto

Minestrone con pesto

Minestrone is a thick mixed vegetable soup using almost any combination of seasonal vegetables. Short pasta or rice may also be added. This version includes pesto sauce.

Ingredients
6¼ cups stock or water, or a combination
   of both
3 tbsp olive oil
1 large onion, finely chopped
1 leek, sliced
2 carrots, finely chopped
1 stalk celery, finely chopped
2 cloves garlic, finely chopped
2 potatoes, peeled and cut into small dice
1 bay leaf
1 sprig fresh thyme, or ¼ tsp dried thyme
   leaves
salt and freshly ground black pepper
¾ cup peas, fresh or frozen
2–3 zucchini, finely chopped
3 medium tomatoes, peeled and finely
   chopped
2 cups cooked or canned beans such as
   cannellini
3 tbsp pesto sauce
freshly grated Parmesan cheese, to serve
serves 6

1 In a medium saucepan, heat the stock or water to simmering.

2 ▲ In a saucepan heat the olive oil. Stir in the onion and leek, and cook for 5–6 minutes, or until the onion softens. Add the carrots, celery and garlic, and cook over moderate heat, stirring often, for another 5 minutes. Add the potatoes and cook for 2–3 minutes more.

3 Pour in the hot stock or water, and stir well. Add the herbs and season with salt and pepper. Bring to a boil, reduce the heat slightly, and cook for 10–12 minutes.

4 Stir in the peas, if fresh, and the zucchini. Simmer for 5 minutes more. Add the frozen peas, if using, and the tomatoes. Cover the pan, and boil for 5–8 minutes.

5 ▲ About 10 minutes before serving the soup, uncover, and stir in the beans. Simmer for 10 minutes. Stir in the pesto sauce. Taste for seasoning. Simmer for another 5 minutes then remove from the heat. Allow the soup to stand for a few minutes, then serve with the grated Parmesan.

Pumpkin Soup

Minestrone di zucca

This beautifully colored soup would be perfect for an autumn dinner.

Ingredients
1 lb piece of peeled pumpkin
¼ cup butter
1 medium onion, finely chopped
3½ cups fresh or canned chicken stock or
   water
2 cups milk
pinch of grated nutmeg
salt and freshly ground black pepper
1½ oz spaghetti, broken into small pieces
6 tbsp freshly grated Parmesan cheese
serves 4

1 Chop the piece of pumpkin into 1 in cubes.

2 ▲ Heat the butter in a saucepan. Add the onion, and cook over moderate heat until it softens, 6–8 minutes. Stir in the pumpkin, and cook for 2–3 minutes more.

3 Add the stock or water, and cook until the pumpkin is soft, about 15 minutes. Remove from the heat.

4 Purée the soup in a blender or food processor. Return it to the pan. Stir in the milk and nutmeg. Season with salt and pepper. Bring the soup back to a boil.

5 Stir the broken spaghetti into the soup. Cook until the pasta is done. Stir in the Parmesan and serve at once.

Broccoli Soup

Zuppa di broccoletti

Around Rome broccoli grows abundantly and is served in this soup with garlic toasts.

Ingredients
1½ lb broccoli spears
7½ cups fresh or canned chicken or
  vegetable stock
salt and freshly ground black pepper
1 tbsp fresh lemon juice
To serve
6 slices white bread
1 large clove garlic, cut in half
freshly grated Parmesan cheese, to serve
  (optional)
serves 6

1 Using a small sharp knife, peel the broccoli stems, starting from the base of the stalks and pulling gently up towards the florets. (The peel comes off very easily.) Chop the broccoli into small chunks.

2 Bring the stock to a boil in a large saucepan. Add the broccoli and simmer for 30 minutes, or until soft.

3 ▲ Purée about half of the soup and mix into the rest of the soup. Season with salt, pepper and lemon juice.

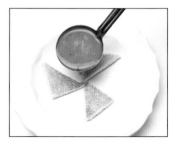

4 ▲ Just before serving, reheat the soup to just below boiling point. Toast the bread, rub with garlic and cut into quarters. Place 3 or 4 pieces of toast in the bottom of each soup plate. Ladle on the soup. Serve at once, with Parmesan if desired.

Tomato and Bread Soup

Pappa al pomodoro

This colorful Florentine recipe was created to use up stale bread. It can be made with very ripe fresh or canned plum tomatoes.

Ingredients
6 tbsp olive oil
small piece of dried chili, crumbled
  (optional)
1½ cups stale coarse white bread, cut
  into 1 in cubes
1 medium onion, finely chopped
2 cloves garlic, finely chopped
1½ lb ripe tomatoes, peeled and
  chopped, or 2 × 14 oz cans peeled
  plum tomatoes, chopped
3 tbsp chopped fresh basil
6¼ cups fresh or canned stock or water,
  or a combination of both
salt and freshly ground black pepper
extra-virgin olive oil, to serve (optional)
serves 4

1 Heat 4 tbsp of the oil in a large saucepan. Add the chili, if using, and stir for 1–2 minutes. Add the bread cubes and cook until golden. Remove to a plate and drain on paper towels.

2 ▲ Add the remaining oil, the onion and garlic, and cook until the onion softens. Stir in the tomatoes, bread and basil. Season with salt. Cook over moderate heat, stirring occasionally, for about 15 minutes.

3 Meanwhile, heat the stock or water to simmering. Add it to the saucepan with the tomato mixture, and mix well. Bring to a boil. Lower the heat slightly and simmer for 20 minutes.

4 ▲ Remove the soup from the heat. Use a fork to mash the tomatoes and the bread together. Season with pepper, and more salt if necessary. Allow to stand for 10 minutes. Just before serving swirl in a little extra-virgin olive oil, if desired.

White Bean Soup

Minestrone di fagioli

A thick purée of cooked dried beans is at the heart of this substantial country soup from Tuscany. It makes a warming winter lunch or supper dish.

Ingredients

1½ cups dried cannellini or other white
   beans
1 bay leaf
5 tbsp olive oil
1 medium onion, finely chopped
1 carrot, finely chopped
1 stalk celery, finely chopped
3 medium tomatoes, peeled and finely
   chopped
2 cloves garlic, finely chopped
1 tsp fresh thyme leaves, or ½ tsp dried
   thyme
3½ cups boiling water
salt and freshly ground black pepper
extra-virgin olive oil, to serve
serves 6

1 ▲ Pick over the beans carefully, discarding any stones or other particles. Soak the beans in a large bowl of cold water overnight. Drain. Place the beans in a large saucepan of water, bring to a boil, and cook for 20 minutes. Drain. Return the beans to the pan, cover with cold water, and bring to a boil again. Add the bay leaf, and cook until the beans are tender, 1–2 hours. Drain again. Remove the bay leaf.

2 Purée about three-quarters of the beans in a food processor, or pass through a food mill, adding a little water if necessary.

3 Heat the oil in a large saucepan. Stir in the onion, and cook until it softens. Add the carrot and celery, and cook for 5 minutes more.

4 ▲ Stir in the tomatoes, garlic and thyme. Cook for 6–8 minutes more, stirring often.

5 ▲ Pour in the boiling water. Stir in the beans and the bean purée. Season with salt and pepper. Simmer for 10–15 minutes. Serve in individual soup bowls, sprinkled with a little extra-virgin olive oil.

Fish Soup

Ciuppin

Liguria is famous for its fish soups. In this one the fish are cooked in a broth with vegetables and then puréed. This soup can also be used to dress pasta.

Ingredients

2 lb mixed fish or fish pieces (such as
    pollock, whiting, red mullet, red or
    white snapper, cod, etc)
6 tbsp olive oil, plus extra to serve
1 medium onion, finely chopped
1 stalk celery, chopped
1 carrot, chopped
4 tbsp chopped fresh parsley
¾ cup dry white wine
3 medium tomatoes, peeled and chopped
2 cloves garlic, finely chopped
6¼ cups boiling water
salt and freshly ground black pepper
rounds of French bread, to serve
serves 6

3 ▲ Pour in the wine, raise the heat, and cook until it reduces by about half. Stir in the tomatoes and garlic. Cook for 3–4 minutes, stirring occasionally. Pour in the boiling water, and bring back to a boil. Cook over moderate heat for 15 minutes.

4 Stir in the fish, and simmer for 10–15 minutes, or until the fish are tender. Season with salt and pepper.

5 ▲ Remove the fish from the soup with a slotted spoon. Discard any bones. Purée in a food processor. Taste for seasoning. If the soup is too thick, add a little more water.

6 To serve, heat the soup to simmering. Toast the rounds of bread, and sprinkle with olive oil. Place 2 or 3 in each soup plate before pouring over the soup.

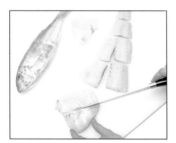

1 ▲ Scale and clean the fish, discarding all innards, but leaving the heads on. Cut into large pieces. Rinse well in cool water.

2 Heat the oil in a large saucepan and add the onion. Cook over low to moderate heat until it begins to soften. Stir in the celery and carrot, and cook for 5 minutes more. Add the parsley.

~ VARIATION ~

To use the soup as a pasta dressing, cook until it reduces to the consistency of a sauce.

Barley and Vegetable Soup
Minestrone d'orzo

This soup comes from the Alto Adige region, in Italy's mountainous north. It is a thick, nourishing and warming winter soup. Serve with crusty bread.

Ingredients
1 cup pearl barley, preferably organic
9 cups fresh or canned beef stock or
    water, or a combination of both
3 tbsp olive oil
2 carrots, finely chopped
1 large onion, finely chopped
2 stalks celery, finely chopped
1 leek, thinly sliced
1 large potato, finely chopped
½ cup diced ham
1 bay leaf
3 tbsp chopped fresh parsley
1 small sprig fresh rosemary
salt and freshly ground black pepper
freshly grated Parmesan cheese, to serve
    (optional)
serves 6–8

1 Pick over the barley, and discard any stones or other particles. Wash it in cold water. Put the barley to soak in cold water for at least 3 hours.

2 Drain the barley and place in a large saucepan with the stock or water. Bring to a boil, lower the heat and simmer for 1 hour. Skim off any scum.

3 ▲ Stir in the oil, all the vegetables and the ham. Add the herbs. If necessary add more water. The ingredients should be covered by at least 1 in. Simmer for 1–1½ hours, or until the vegetables and barley are very tender.

4 ▲ Taste for seasoning, adding salt and pepper as necessary. Serve hot with grated Parmesan, if desired.

~ VARIATION ~

An excellent vegetarian version of this soup can be made by using vegetable stock instead of beef stock, and omitting the ham.

Rice and Broad Bean Soup
Minestra di riso e fave

This thick soup makes the most of fresh broad beans while they are in season. It works well with frozen beans for the rest of the year.

Ingredients
2 lb broad beans in their pods, or 14 oz
    shelled frozen broad beans, thawed
6 tbsp olive oil
1 medium onion, finely chopped
salt and freshly ground black pepper
2 medium tomatoes, peeled and finely
    chopped
1 cup risotto or other non-parboiled rice
2 tbsp butter
4 cups boiling water
freshly grated Parmesan cheese, to serve
    (optional)
serves 4

1 ▲ Shell the beans if they are fresh. Bring a large pan of water to a boil, and blanch the beans, fresh or frozen, for 3–4 minutes. Rinse under cold water, and peel off the skins.

2 Heat the oil in a large saucepan. Add the onion, and cook over low to moderate heat until it softens. Stir in the beans, and cook for about 5 minutes, stirring often to coat them with the oil. Season with salt and pepper. Add the tomatoes, and cook for 5 minutes more, stirring often.

3 Stir in the rice. After 1–2 minutes add the butter, and stir until it melts. Pour in the water, a little at a time, until the whole amount has been added. Taste for seasoning. Continue cooking the soup until the rice is tender. Serve hot, with grated Parmesan if desired.

Pasta and Dried Bean Soup

Pasta e fagioli

This peasant soup is very thick. In Italy it is made with dried or fresh beans, never canned, and served hot or at room temperature.

Ingredients

1½ cups dried borlotti or cannellini beans
1 × 14 oz can plum tomatoes, chopped, with their juice
3 cloves garlic, crushed
2 bay leaves
pinch coarsely ground black pepper
6 tbsp olive oil, plus extra to serve (optional)
3½ cups water
2 tsp salt
2¼ cups ditalini, pastina, or other small pasta
3 tbsp chopped fresh parsley
freshly grated Parmesan cheese, to serve
serves 4–6

1 Soak the beans in water overnight. Rinse and drain well.

2 Place the beans in a large saucepan and cover with water. Bring to a boil and cook for 10 minutes. Rinse and drain again.

3 ▲ Return the beans to the pan. Add enough water to cover them by 1 in. Stir in the coarsely chopped tomatoes with their juice, the garlic, bay leaves, black pepper and the oil. Simmer for 1½–2 hours, or until the beans are tender. If necessary, add more water.

4 ▲ Remove the bay leaves. Pass about half of the bean mixture through a food mill, or purée in a food processor. Stir into the pan with the remaining bean mixture. Add the water, and bring the soup to a boil.

5 Add the salt and the pasta. Stir well, and cook until the pasta is just done. Stir in the parsley. Allow to stand for at least 10 minutes before serving. Serve with grated Parmesan passed separately. In Italy a little olive oil is poured into each serving.

Pasta and Lentil Soup

Pasta e lenticchie

The small brown lentils which are grown in central Italy are usually used in this wholesome soup, but green lentils may be substituted if preferred.

Ingredients

1 cup dried green or brown lentils, picked over
6 tbsp olive oil
¼ cup ham or salt pork, cut into small dice
1 medium onion, finely chopped
1 stalk celery, finely chopped
1 carrot, finely chopped
9 cups chicken stock or water, or a combination of both
1 leaf fresh sage or ⅛ tsp dried sage
1 sprig fresh thyme or ¼ tsp dried thyme
salt and freshly ground black pepper
2½ cups ditalini, pastina, or other small soup pasta

serves 4–6

1 ▲ Carefully check the lentils for small pitts. Place them in a bowl, covered with cold water, and soak for 2–3 hours. Rinse and drain well.

2 ▲ In a large saucepan, heat the oil and sauté the ham or salt pork for 2–3 minutes. Add the onion, and cook gently until it softens.

3 ▲ Stir in the celery and carrot, and cook for 5 minutes more, stirring frequently. Add the lentils, and stir to coat them in the fats.

4 ▲ Pour in the stock or water and the herbs, and bring the soup to a boil. Cook over moderate heat for about 1 hour or until the lentils are tender. Add salt and pepper to taste.

5 Stir in the pasta, and cook it until it is just done. Allow the soup to stand for a few minutes before serving.

Pasta and Chickpea Soup

Pasta e ceci

Another thick soup from central Italy. The addition of a sprig of fresh rosemary provides a typically Mediterranean flavor.

Ingredients
1 cup dried chickpeas
3 cloves garlic, peeled
1 bay leaf
6 tbsp olive oil
pinch of freshly ground black pepper
¼ cup salt pork, pancetta or bacon, diced
1 sprig fresh rosemary
2½ cups water
2 cups ditalini, tubetti, or other short
    hollow pasta
salt, to taste
freshly grated Parmesan cheese, to serve
    (optional)
serves 4–6

2 ▲ Return the chickpeas to the pan. Add water to cover, 1 clove of garlic, the bay leaf, 3 tbsp of the oil and the ground pepper.

4 ▲ Sauté the diced pork gently in the remaining oil with the rosemary and 2 cloves of garlic until just golden. Discard the rosemary and garlic.

1 ▲ Soak the chickpeas in water overnight. Rinse well and drain. Place the chickpeas in a large saucepan with water to cover. Boil for 15 minutes. Rinse and drain.

3 ▲ Simmer until tender, about 2 hours, adding more water as necessary. Remove the bay leaf. Pass about half the chickpeas through a food mill or purée in a food processor with a few tablespoons of the cooking liquid. Return the purée to the pan with the rest of the peas and the remaining cooking water.

5 ▲ Stir the pork with its oils into the chickpea mixture.

~ COOK'S TIP ~

Allow the soup to stand for about 10 minutes before serving. This will allow the flavor and texture to develop.

6 ▲ Add 2½ cups of water to the chickpeas, and bring to a boil. Correct the seasoning if necessary. Stir in the pasta, and cook until just *al dente*. Pass the Parmesan separately, if desired.

VEGETABLES

The colors and flavors of the Mediterranean are at the heart of this distinctive collection of vegetable dishes. Stuffed artichokes, baked fennel and grilled radicchio are some of its hearty delights.

Stuffed Artichokes

Carciofi ripieni

Artichokes grow almost wild in southern Italy and they are cooked in many different ways. In this recipe the artichokes are stuffed and baked whole.

Ingredients
1 lemon
6 large globe artichokes
For the stuffing
2 slices white bread, crusts removed
    (about 2 oz)
3 anchovy fillets, finely chopped
2 cloves garlic, finely chopped
2 tbsp capers, rinsed and finely chopped
3 tbsp finely chopped fresh parsley
4 tbsp plain dry breadcrumbs
4 tbsp olive oil
salt and freshly ground black pepper
For baking
1 clove garlic, cut into 3 or 4 pieces
1 sprig fresh parsley
3 tbsp olive oil
serves 6

1 Prepare the stuffing. Soak the white bread in a little water for 5 minutes. Squeeze dry. Place in a bowl with the other stuffing ingredients and mix.

2 ▲ Squeeze the lemon, and put the juice and the squeezed halves in a large bowl of cold water. Wash the artichokes and prepare them one at a time. Cut off only the tip from the stem. Peel the stem with a small knife, pulling upwards towards the leaves. Pull off the small leaves around the stem, and continue snapping off the upper part of the dark outer leaves until you reach the taller inner leaves. Cut off the topmost part of these leaves with a sharp knife.

3 ▲ Open the artichoke slightly by spreading the leaves apart to get at the inner bristly "choke". Cut around it with the knife, and scrape it out with a small spoon. This forms a cavity inside the artichoke leaves. As soon as each artichoke has been prepared, place it in the bowl of acidulated water. This will prevent it from darkening. Preheat the oven to 375°F.

4 ▲ Place the garlic and the parsley leaves in a baking dish large enough to hold the artichokes upright in one layer. Pour in cold water to a depth of ½ inch. Remove the artichokes from the bowl, drain quickly, and fill the cavities with the stuffing. Place the artichokes upside down in the dish. Pour a little oil over each. Cover the dish tightly with foil. Bake for about 1 hour, or until tender.

Asparagus with Eggs

Asparagi alla milanese

The addition of fried eggs and grated Parmesan turns asparagus into something special.

Peeling enables the asparagus to cook evenly, and makes the whole spear edible.

Ingredients

1 lb fresh asparagus
5 tbsp butter
4 eggs
4 tbsp freshly grated Parmesan cheese
salt and freshly ground black pepper
serves 4

4 ▲ As soon as the asparagus is cooked, remove it from the water with two slotted spoons. Place it on a cake rack covered with a clean dish towel to drain. Divide the spears between warmed individual serving plates. Place a fried egg on each, and sprinkle with the grated Parmesan.

5 ▲ Melt the remaining butter in the frying pan. As soon as it is bubbling pour it over the cheese and eggs on the asparagus. Serve at once with salt and pepper.

1 ▲ Cut off any woody ends from the asparagus. Peel the lower half of the asparagus spears by inserting a knife under the thick skin at the base, and pulling upwards towards the tip. Wash the asparagus in cold water.

2 Bring a large pan of water to a boil. Boil the asparagus until just tender when pierced with a knife.

3 ▲ While the asparagus is cooking, melt about a third of the butter in a frying pan. When it is bubbling, gently break in the eggs one at a time, and cook them until the whites have set, but the yolks are still soft.

Stewed Artichokes

Carciofi in umido

Artichokes are eaten in many ways in Italy, sometimes sliced paper-thin and eaten raw as a salad, sometimes cut up and stewed lightly with garlic, parsley and wine, as in this recipe.

Ingredients
1 lemon
4 large or 6 small globe artichokes
2 tbsp butter
4 tbsp olive oil
2 cloves garlic, finely chopped
4 tbsp chopped fresh parsley
salt and freshly ground black pepper
3 tbsp water
6 tbsp milk
6 tbsp white wine
serves 6

1 Squeeze the lemon, and put the juice and the squeezed halves in a large bowl of cold water. Wash the artichokes and prepare them one at a time. Cut off only the tip from the stem. Peel the stem with a small knife, pulling upwards towards the leaves. Pull off the small leaves around the stem, and continue snapping off the upper part of the dark outer leaves until you reach the taller inner leaves.

2 ▲ Slice the topmost part of the leaves off. Cut the artichoke into 4 or 6 segments.

3 Cut out the bristly "choke" from each segment. Place in the acidulated water to prevent the artichokes from darkening while you prepare the rest.

4 Blanch the artichokes in a large pan of rapidly boiling water for 4–5 minutes. Drain.

5 ▲ Heat the butter and olive oil in a large saucepan. Add the garlic and parsley, and cook for 2–3 minutes. Stir in the artichokes. Season with salt and pepper. Add the water and the milk, and cook for about 10 minutes, or until the liquid has evaporated. Stir in the wine, cover and cook until the artichokes are tender. Serve hot or at room temperature.

Green Beans with Tomatoes

Fagiolini verdi con pomodori

This dish is particularly good when fresh tomatoes are used.

Ingredients
1 lb fresh green beans
3 tbsp olive oil
1 medium onion, preferably red, very finely sliced
12 oz plum tomatoes, fresh or canned, peeled and finely chopped
½ cup water
salt and freshly ground black pepper
5–6 leaves of fresh basil torn into pieces
serves 4–6

1 Snap or cut the stem ends off the beans, and wash well in plenty of cold water. Drain.

2 ▲ Heat the oil in a large frying pan with a cover. Add the onion slices and cook until just soft, 5–6 minutes. Add the tomatoes and cook over moderate heat until they soften, about 6–8 minutes. Stir in the water. Season with salt and pepper, and add the basil.

3 ▲ Stir in the beans, turning them in the pan to coat with the sauce. Cover the pan, and cook over moderate heat until tender, about 15–20 minutes. Stir occasionally, and add a little more water if the sauce dries out too much. Serve hot or cold.

Eggplant Parmesan

Parmigiana di melanzane

This famous dish is a speciality of Italy's southern regions.

Ingredients
2 lb eggplants
flour, for coating
oil, for frying
⅓ cup freshly grated Parmesan cheese
2 cups mozzarella cheese, sliced very
    thinly
salt and freshly ground black pepper
For the tomato sauce
4 tbsp olive oil
1 medium onion, very finely chopped
1 clove garlic, finely chopped
1 lb tomatoes, fresh or canned, chopped,
    with their juice
salt and freshly ground black pepper
a few leaves fresh basil or sprigs parsley
serves 4–6

1 Wash the eggplants. Cut into rounds about ½ inch wide, sprinkle with salt, and leave to drain for about 1 hour.

2 ▲ Meanwhile make the tomato sauce. Heat the oil in a medium saucepan. Add the onion, and cook over moderate heat until it is translucent, 5–8 minutes. Stir in the garlic and the tomatoes (add 3 tbsp of water if you are using fresh tomatoes). Season with salt and pepper. Add the basil or parsley. Cook for 20–30 minutes. Purée in a food mill or a food processor.

3 Pat the eggplant slices dry with paper towels. Coat lightly in flour. Heat a little oil in a large frying pan (preferably non-stick). Add one layer of eggplant, and cook over low to moderate heat with the pan covered until soft. Turn, and cook on the other side. Remove from the pan, and repeat with the remaining slices.

4 Preheat the oven to 350°F. Grease a wide shallow baking dish or pan. Spread a little tomato sauce in the bottom. Cover with a layer of eggplant. Sprinkle with a few teaspoons of Parmesan, season with salt and pepper, and cover with a layer of mozzarella. Spoon on some tomato sauce. Repeat until all the ingredients are used up, ending with a covering of tomato sauce and a sprinkling of Parmesan. Sprinkle with a little olive oil, and bake for about 45 minutes.

Sweet and Sour Eggplant

Caponata

This delicious Sicilian dish combines eggplant and celery in a piquant sauce.

Ingredients
1½ lb eggplants
2 tbsp olive oil
1 medium onion, finely sliced
1 clove garlic, finely chopped
1 × 8 oz can plum tomatoes, peeled and
    finely chopped
½ cup white wine vinegar
2 tbsp sugar
salt and freshly ground black pepper
tender central stalks of a head of celery
    (about 6 oz)
2 tbsp capers, rinsed
½ cup green olives, pitted
oil, for deep-frying
2 tbsp chopped fresh parsley
serves 4

1 Wash the eggplants and cut into small cubes. Sprinkle with salt, and leave to drain in a colander for 1 hour.

2 ▲ Heat the oil in a large saucepan. Stir in the onion, and cook until soft. Stir in the garlic and tomatoes, and fry over moderate heat for 10 minutes. Stir in the vinegar, sugar and pepper. Simmer until the sauce reduces, 10 more. Blanch the celery stalks in boiling water until tender. Drain, and chop into 1 in pieces. Add to the sauce with the capers and olives.

3 ▲ Pat the eggplant cubes dry with paper towels. Heat the oil to 360°F, and deep-fry the eggplant in batches until golden. Drain on paper towels.

4 Add the eggplant to the sauce. Stir gently and season. Stir in the parsley. Allow to stand for 30 minutes. Serve at room temperature.

Carrots with Marsala

Carote al marsala

The sweet flavor of marsala goes surprisingly well with carrots in this Sicilian dish.

Ingredients
4 tbsp butter
1 lb carrots, thinly sliced
1 tsp sugar
½ tsp salt
¼ cup marsala
serves 4

1 Melt the butter in a medium saucepan, and add the carrots. Stir well to coat with the butter. Add the sugar and salt, and mix well.

2 ▲ Stir in the marsala, and simmer for 4–5 minutes.

3 ▲ Pour in enough water to barely cover the carrots. Cover the pan, and cook over low to moderate heat until the carrots are tender. Remove the cover, and cook until the liquids reduce almost completely. Serve hot.

Broccoli with Oil and Garlic

Broccoletti saltati con aglio

This is a very simple way of transforming steamed or blanched broccoli into a succulent Mediterranean dish. Peeling the broccoli stalks is easy, and allows for even cooking.

Ingredients
2 lb fresh broccoli
6 tbsp olive oil
2–3 cloves garlic, finely chopped
salt and freshly ground black pepper
serves 6

1 ▲ Wash the broccoli. Cut off any woody parts at the base of the stems. Use a small sharp knife to peel the broccoli stems. Cut any very long or wide stalks in half.

2 ▲ Boil water in the bottom of a saucepan equipped with a steamer, or bring a large pan of water to a boil. If steaming the broccoli, put it in the steamer and cover tightly. Cook for 8–12 minutes or until the stems are just tender when pierced with the point of a knife. Remove from the heat. If blanching, drop the broccoli into the pan of boiling water and blanch until just tender, 5–6 minutes. Drain.

3 ▲ In a frying pan large enough to hold all the broccoli pieces, gently heat the oil with the garlic. When the garlic is light golden (do not let it brown or it will be bitter) add the broccoli, and cook over moderate heat for 3–4 minutes, turning carefully to coat it with the hot oil. Season with salt and pepper. Serve hot or cold.

Meat-stuffed Cabbage Rolls

Involtini di verza ripieni di carne

Stuffed cabbage leaves are a good way of using up cooked meats. These rolls are quite substantial, and make a satisfying luncheon dish.

Ingredients

1 head Savoy cabbage
⅔ cup white bread
milk, to soak bread
1½ cups cold meat, very finely chopped,
    or fresh lean ground beef
1 egg
2 tbsp finely chopped fresh parsley
1 clove garlic, finely chopped
½ cup freshly grated Parmesan cheese
pinch of grated nutmeg
salt and freshly ground black pepper
5 tbsp olive oil
1 medium onion, finely chopped
1 cup dry white wine
serves 4–5

2 ▲ Cut the crusts from the bread, and discard. Soak the bread in a little milk for about 5 minutes. Squeeze out the excess moisture with your hands.

3 ▲ In a mixing bowl combine the chopped or minced meat with the egg and soaked bread. Stir in the parsley, garlic and Parmesan. Season with nutmeg, salt and pepper.

1 ▲ Cut the leaves from the cabbage. Save the innermost part for soup. Blanch the leaves a few at a time in a large pan of boiling water for 4–5 minutes. Refresh under cold water. Spread the leaves out on clean dish towels to dry.

~ VARIATION ~

Serve the rolls with a tomato sauce, spooned over just before serving.

4 ▲ Divide any very large cabbage leaves in half, discarding the rib. Lay the leaves out on a flat surface. Form

little sausage-shaped mounds of stuffing, and place them at the edge of each leaf. Roll up the leaves, tucking the ends in as you roll. Squeeze each roll lightly in the palm of your hand to help the leaves to stick.

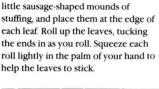

5 ▲ In a large, shallow, flameproof casserole or deep frying pan large enough to hold all the cabbage rolls in one layer, heat the olive oil. Add the onion, and cook gently until it softens. Raise the heat slightly, and add the cabbage rolls, turning them over carefully with a large spoon as they begin to cook.

6 ▲ Pour in half of the wine. Cook over low to moderate heat until the wine has evaporated. Add the rest of the wine, cover the pan, and cook for 10–15 minutes more. Remove the cover, and cook until all the liquid has evaporated. Remove from the heat, and allow to rest for about 5 minutes before serving.

Broad Bean Purée with Ham

Purea di fave con prosciutto

Peeling broad beans leaves them tender and sweet. They go particularly well with the saltiness of prosciutto crudo in this Tuscan combination.

Ingredients
2 lb fresh broad beans in their pods, or
    14 oz shelled broad beans, thawed if
    frozen
1 medium onion, finely chopped
2 small potatoes, peeled and diced
¼ cup prosciutto crudo
3 tbsp extra-virgin olive oil
salt and freshly ground black pepper
serves 4

1 Place the shelled beans in a saucepan and cover with water. Bring to a boil and cook for 5 minutes. Drain. When they are cool enough to handle, peel the beans.

2 ▲ Place the peeled beans in a saucepan with the onion and potatoes. Add enough water just to cover the vegetables. Bring to a boil. Lower the heat slightly, cover, and simmer until the vegetables are very soft, 15–20 minutes. Check occasionally that all the water has not evaporated. If necessary add a few tablespoons more.

3 Chop the ham into very small dice. Heat the oil and sauté until the ham is just golden.

4 ▲ Mash or purée the bean mixture. Return it to the pan. If it is very moist, cook it over moderate heat until it reduces slightly. Stir in the oil with the ham. Season and cook for 2 minutes.

Deep-fried Cauliflower

Cavolfiore fritto

Deep-frying is very popular in Italy, and everything from cheese to fruit may be fried. The cauliflower may be eaten as a side dish or as an antipasto.

Ingredients
1 large cauliflower
1 egg
salt and freshly ground black pepper
scant 1 cup flour
¾ cup dry white wine
oil, for deep-frying
serves 4

1 Soak the cauliflower in a bowl of salted water. In a mixing bowl, beat the egg. Season and beat in the flour. The mixture will be very thick. Add the wine. If necessary add more to make a fairly runny batter. Cover, and allow to rest for 30 minutes.

2 Steam or boil the cauliflower until just tender – do not overcook. Cut it into small florets when cool.

3 ▲ Heat the oil until a small piece of bread sizzles as soon as it is dropped in (about 360°F). Dip each cauliflower piece into the batter before deep-frying it until golden.

4 ▲ Remove from the oil with a slotted spoon and drain on paper towels. Sprinkle lightly with salt and serve hot.

Baked Fennel with Parmesan Cheese   *Finocchio gratinato*

Fennel is widely eaten in Italy, both raw and cooked. It is delicious married with the sharpness of Parmesan cheese in this quick and simple dish.

Ingredients
2 lb fennel bulbs, washed and cut in half
4 tbsp butter
⅓ cup freshly grated Parmesan cheese
serves 4–6

2 ▲ Cut the fennel bulbs lengthwise into 4 or 6 pieces. Place them in a buttered baking dish.

3 ▲ Dot with butter. Sprinkle with the grated Parmesan. Bake in the hot oven until the cheese is golden brown, about 20 minutes. Serve at once.

1 ▲ Cook the fennel in a large pan of boiling water until just tender and not at all mushy. Drain. Preheat the oven to 400°F.

~ VARIATION ~

For a more substantial version of this dish, sprinkle 3 oz chopped ham over the fennel before topping with the cheese.

Roast Mushroom Caps   *Funghi arrosti*

Hunting for edible wild mushrooms is one of the Italians' great passions. The most prized are porcini which grow in forests, but are available here fresh in the markets in fall.

Ingredients
4 large mushroom caps, such as porcini
    or portobello
2 cloves garlic, chopped
3 tbsp chopped fresh parsley
salt and freshly ground black pepper
extra-virgin olive oil, for sprinkling
serves 4

1 Preheat the oven to 375°F. Carefully wipe the mushrooms clean with a damp cloth or paper towel. Cut off the stems. (Save them for soup if they are not too woody). Oil a baking dish large enough to hold the mushrooms in one layer.

2 ▲ Place the mushroom caps in the dish, smooth side down. Mix together the chopped garlic and parsley and sprinkle on the caps.

3 ▲ Season the mushrooms with salt and pepper. Sprinkle the parsley stuffing with oil. Bake for 20–25 minutes. Serve at once.

Zucchine with Sun-dried Tomatoes   *Zucchine con pomodori*

One way to preserve tomatoes for winter is to dry them in the sun, as they do all over southern Italy. These tomatoes have a concentrated, sweet flavor that goes well with zucchine.

Ingredients
10 sun-dried tomatoes, dry or preserved
    in oil and drained
¾ cup warm water
5 tbsp olive oil
1 large onion, finely sliced
2 cloves garlic, finely chopped
2 lb zucchine, cut into thin strips
salt and freshly ground black pepper
serves 6

3 ▲ Stir in the garlic and the zucchine. Cook for about 5 minutes, continuing to stir the mixture.

4 ▲ Stir in the tomatoes and their soaking liquid. Season with salt and pepper. Raise the heat slightly and cook until the zucchine are just tender. Serve hot or cold.

1 ▲ Slice the tomatoes into thin strips. Place in a bowl with the warm water. Allow to stand for 20 minutes.

2 ▲ In a large frying pan or saucepan, heat the oil and stir in the onion. Cook over low to moderate heat until it softens but does not brown.

Stuffed Onions

Cipolle ripiene

These savory onions make a satisfying dish for a light lunch or supper. Small onions could be stuffed and served as an accompaniment to a meat dish.

Ingredients
6 large onions
scant ½ cup ham, cut into small dice
1 egg
½ cup dry breadcrumbs
3 tbsp finely chopped fresh parsley
1 clove garlic, finely chopped
pinch of grated nutmeg
¾ cup grated cheese, such as Parmesan
  or Romano
6 tbsp olive oil
salt and freshly ground black pepper
serves 6

1 Peel the onions without cutting through the base. Cook them in a large pan of boiling water for about 20 minutes. Drain, and refresh in plenty of cold water.

2 ▲ Using a small sharp knife, cut around and scoop out the central section. Remove about half the inside (save it for soup). Lightly salt the empty cavities, and leave the onions to drain upside down.

3 ▲ Preheat the oven to 400°F. In a small bowl, beat the ham into the egg. Stir in the breadcrumbs, parsley, garlic, nutmeg and all but 3 tbsp of the grated cheese. Add 3 tbsp of the oil, and season with salt and pepper.

4 Pat the insides of the onions dry with paper towels. Stuff them using a small spoon. Arrange the onions in one layer in an oiled baking dish.

5 ▲ Sprinkle the tops with the remaining cheese, and sprinkle with oil. Bake for 45 minutes, or until the onions are tender and golden on top.

~ VARIATION ~

For a vegetarian version, replace the ham with chopped olives.

Aromatic Stewed Mushrooms

Funghi trifolati

This dish from Piedmont combines both field and cultivated mushrooms, which give a balanced but not overwhelming flavor.

Ingredients
1½ lb firm fresh mushrooms, field and
    cultivated
6 tbsp olive oil
2 cloves garlic, finely chopped
salt and freshly ground black pepper
3 tbsp chopped fresh parsley
serves 6

1 ▲ Clean the mushrooms carefully by wiping them with a damp cloth or paper towels.

2 ▲ Cut off the woody tips of the stems and discard. Slice the stems and caps fairly thickly.

3 ▲ Heat the oil in a large frying pan. Stir in the garlic and, after about 1 minute, the mushrooms. Cook for 8–10 minutes, stirring occasionally. Season with salt and pepper, and stir in the parsley. Cook for 5 minutes more, and serve at once.

Sautéed Peas with Ham

Piselli alla fiorentina

When fresh peas are in season, they can be stewed with a little ham and onion and served as a substantial side dish.

Ingredients
3 tbsp olive oil
½ cup pancetta or ham, finely diced
3 tbsp finely chopped onion
2 lb whole peas (about 11 oz shelled) or
    10 oz frozen petit pois, thawed
2–3 tbsp water
salt and freshly ground black pepper
a few leaves fresh mint or sprigs parsley
additional parsley or mint to garnish
    (optional)
serves 4

1 Heat the oil in a medium saucepan, and sauté the pancetta or ham and onion for 2–3 minutes.

2 ▲ Stir in the shelled fresh or thawed frozen peas. Add the water. Season with salt and pepper and mix well to coat with the oil.

3 ▲ Add the fresh herbs, cover, and cook over moderate heat until tender. This may take from 5 minutes for sweet fresh peas, to 15 for tougher, older peas. Serve as a side dish to meat dishes or frittate.

Stuffed Peppers

Peperoni ripieni

Sweet peppers can be stuffed and baked with many different fillings, from leftover cooked vegetables to rice or pasta. Blanching the peppers first helps to make them tender.

Ingredients

6 medium to large peppers, any color
scant 1 cup rice
4 tbsp olive oil
1 large onion, finely chopped
3 anchovy fillets, chopped
2 cloves garlic, finely chopped
3 medium tomatoes, peeled and cut into small dice
4 tbsp white wine
3 tbsp finely chopped fresh parsley
½ cup mozzarella cheese, cut into small dice
6 tbsp freshly grated Parmesan cheese
salt and freshly ground black pepper
Basic Tomato Sauce, to serve (optional)
serves 6

2 ▲ Boil the rice according to the instructions on the package, but drain and rinse it in cold water 3 minutes before the recommended cooking time has elapsed. Drain again.

1 ▲ Cut the tops off the peppers. Scoop out the seeds and fibrous insides. Blanch the peppers and their tops in a large pan of boiling water for 3–4 minutes. Remove, and stand upside down on racks to drain.

3 ▲ In a large frying pan, heat the oil and sauté the onion until soft. Stir in the anchovy pieces and the garlic, and mash them. Add the tomatoes, and the wine, and cook for 5 minutes.

4 ▲ Preheat the oven to 375°F. Remove the tomato mixture from the heat. Stir in the rice, parsley, mozzarella and 4 tbsp of the Parmesan cheese. Season the mixture with salt and pepper.

5 ▲ Pat the insides of the peppers dry with paper towels. Sprinkle with salt and pepper. Stuff the peppers. Sprinkle the tops with the remaining Parmesan, and sprinkle with a little oil.

6 ▲ Arrange the peppers in a shallow baking dish. Pour in enough water to come ½ inch up the sides of the peppers. Bake for 25 minutes. Serve at once, with tomato sauce if desired. These peppers are also good served at room temperature.

~ COOK'S TIP ~

Choose peppers with sturdy, even bases, so they will stand on end unsupported. This will make them easier to cook and serve.

Stewed Peppers

Peperonata

This dish originated in the south of Italy, but has become a popular favorite everywhere. It can be eaten as a side dish or appetizer, and makes a delicious stuffing for a frittata.

Ingredients
4–5 very ripe peppers, preferably red or
     yellow, about 750 g/1½ lb
60 ml/4 tbsp olive oil
2 medium onions, thinly sliced
3 cloves garlic, finely chopped
350 g/12 oz plum tomatoes, peeled,
     seeded and chopped
salt and freshly ground black pepper
a few fresh basil leaves
serves 6

1 Wash the peppers. Cut them into quarters, removing the stems and seeds. Slice them into thin strips.

2 ▲ In a large heavy saucepan, heat the oil and sauté the onions until soft (covering the pan will prevent the onions from browning). Add the peppers, and cook for 5–8 minutes over moderate heat, stirring frequently.

3 ▲ Stir in the garlic and tomatoes. Cover the pan, and cook for about 25 minutes, stirring occasionally. The peppers should be soft, but should still hold their shape. Season, tear the basil leaves into pieces, and stir into the peppers. Serve hot or cold.

Grilled Radicchio and Zucchine

Verdure ai ferri

In Italy radicchio is often eaten grilled or barbecued. It is delicious and very easy to prepare.

Ingredients
2–3 firm heads of radicchio, round or long
     type
4 medium zucchine
90 ml/6 tbsp olive oil
salt and freshly ground black pepper
serves 4

2 ▲ Cut the zucchine into 1 cm/ ½ inch diagonal slices.

3 ▲ When the grill or barbecue is hot, brush the vegetables all over with the oil, and sprinkle with salt and pepper. Cook for 4–5 minutes on each side. Serve alone or as an accompaniment to grilled fish or meats.

1 ▲ Preheat the grill, or prepare a barbecue. Cut the radicchio in half through the root section or base. If necessary, wash in cold water. Drain.

Potatoes Baked with Tomatoes

Patate e pomodori al forno

This simple, hearty dish from the south of Italy is best when tomatoes are in season, but can also be made with canned plum tomatoes.

Ingredients

2 large red or yellow onions, thinly sliced
2 lb potatoes, peeled and thinly sliced
1 lb tomatoes, fresh or canned, sliced,
    with their juice
6 tbsp olive oil
1 cup freshly grated Parmesan or
    Romano
salt and freshly ground black pepper
a few leaves fresh basil
¼ cup water
serves 6

1 Preheat the oven to 350°F. Brush a large baking dish generously with oil.

2 ▲ Arrange a layer of onions in the dish, followed by layers of potatoes and tomatoes. Pour on a little of the oil, and sprinkle with the cheese. Season with salt and pepper.

layer of potatoes and tomatoes. Tear the basil leaves into pieces, and add them here and there among the vegetables. Sprinkle the top with cheese, and a little oil.

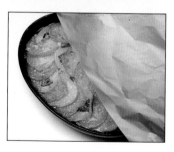

3 ▲ Repeat until the vegetables are used up, ending with an overlapping

4 ▲ Pour on the water. Bake for 1 hour, or until tender.

5 ▲ If the top begins to brown too much, place a sheet of foil or a flat cookie sheet on top of the dish. Serve hot.

Tomatoes with Pasta Stuffing

Pomodori ripieni di pasta

Tomatoes are one of Italy's staple foods, appearing in more than three-quarters of all Italian savory dishes. They can be baked with various stuffings. This one comes from the south.

Ingredients

8 large tomatoes, firm and ripe
1¼ cups small soup pasta
8 black olives, pitted and finely chopped
3 tbsp finely chopped mixed fresh herbs, such as chives, parsley, basil and thyme
4 tbsp grated Parmesan cheese
4 tbsp olive oil
salt and freshly ground black pepper
serves 4

3 ▲ Preheat the oven to 375°F. Combine the pasta with the remaining ingredients in a bowl. Stir in the drained tomato pulp. Season with salt and pepper.

4 ▲ Stuff the tomatoes, and replace the tops. Arange them in one layer in a well-oiled baking dish. Bake for 15–20 minutes. Peel off the skins, if desired. Serve hot or at room temperature.

1 ▲ Wash the tomatoes. Slice off the tops, and scoop out the pulp with a small spoon. Chop the pulp and turn the tomatoes upside down on a rack to drain.

2 ▲ Place the pulp in a strainer, and allow the juices to drain off. Meanwhile, boil the pasta in a pan of boiling salted water. Drain it 2 minutes before the recommended cooking time elapses.

Tomato and Bread Salad

Panzanella

This salad is a traditional peasant dish from Tuscany which was created to use up bread that was several days old. It is best made with sun-ripened tomatoes.

Ingredients
3½ cups stale white or brown bread or
   rolls
4 large tomatoes
1 large red onion, or 6 scallions
a few leaves fresh basil, to garnish
For the dressing
4 tbsp extra-virgin olive oil
2 tbsp white wine vinegar
salt and freshly ground black pepper
serves 4

1 Cut the bread or rolls into thick slices. Place in a shallow bowl, and soak with cold water. Leave for at least 30 minutes.

2 ▲ Cut the tomatoes into chunks. Place in a serving bowl. Finely slice the onion or scallions, and add them to the tomatoes. Squeeze as much water out of the bread as possible, and add it to the vegetables.

3 ▲ Make a dressing with the oil and vinegar. Season with salt and pepper. Pour it over the salad and mix well. Decorate with the basil leaves. Allow to stand in a cool place for at least 2 hours before serving.

Broiled Pepper Salad

Insalata di peperoni

This colorful salad is a southern Italian creation: all the ingredients are sun-lovers which thrive in the hot, dry Mezzogiorno.

Ingredients
4 large peppers, red or yellow or a
   combination of both
2 tbsp capers in salt, vinegar, or brine,
   rinsed
18–20 black or green olives
For the dressing
6 tbsp extra-virgin olive oil
2 cloves garlic, finely chopped
2 tbsp balsamic or wine vinegar
salt and freshly ground black pepper
serves 6

1 Place the peppers under a hot broiler, and turn occasionally until they are black and blistered on all sides. Remove from the heat and place in a paper bag. Leave for 5 minutes.

2 ▲ Peel the peppers, then cut into quarters. Remove the stems and seeds.

3 Cut the peppers into strips, and arrange them in a serving dish. Distribute the capers and olives evenly over the peppers.

4 ▲ For the dressing, mix the oil and garlic together in a small bowl, crushing the garlic with a spoon to release as much flavor as possible. Mix in the vinegar, and season with salt and pepper. Pour over the dressing, mix well, and allow to stand for at least 30 minutes before serving.

Artichoke Salad with Eggs

Insalata di carciofi con uova

Artichoke bottoms are best when cut from fresh artichokes, but can also be bought frozen.
This salad is easily assembled for a light lunch.

Ingredients

4 large artichokes, or 4 frozen artichoke
    bottoms, thawed
½ lemon
4 eggs, hard-boiled and shelled
For the mayonnaise
1 egg yolk
2 tsp Dijon mustard
1 tbsp white wine vinegar
salt and freshly ground black pepper
1 cup olive or vegetable oil
a few sprigs fresh parsley
serves 4

3 ▲ Make the mayonnaise. Combine the egg yolk, mustard and vinegar in a mixing bowl. Add salt and pepper to taste. Add the oil in a thin stream while beating vigorously with a wire whisk. When the mixture is thick and smooth, stir in the parsley. Blend well. Cover and refrigerate until needed.

4 ▲ Pull the leaves off the fresh artichokes. Cut the stems off level with the base. Scrape the hairy "choke" off with a knife or spoon.

5 Assemble the salad by cutting the eggs and artichokes into wedges. Arrange on a serving plate, and serve garnished with the mayonnaise.

1 ▲ If using fresh artichokes, wash them. Squeeze the lemon, and put the juice and the squeezed half in a bowl of cold water. Prepare the artichokes one at a time. Cut off only the tip from the stem. Peel the stem with a small knife, pulling upwards towards the leaves. Pull off the small leaves around the stem, and continue snapping off the upper part of the dark outer leaves until you reach the taller inner leaves. Cut the tops off the leaves with a sharp knife. Place in the acidulated water. Repeat with the other artichokes.

2 Boil or steam fresh artichokes until just tender (when a leaf comes away quite easily when pulled). Cook frozen artichoke bottoms according to package instructions. Allow to cool.

Fennel and Orange Salad   *Insalata di finocchio con arancio*

In seventeenth-century Italy fennel was often served at the end of the meal, sprinkled with salt. This refreshing salad originated in Sicily.

Ingredients
2 large fennel bulbs (about 1½ lb)
2 sweet oranges
2 scallions, to garnish
For the dressing
4 tbsp extra-virgin olive oil
2 tbsp fresh lemon juice
salt and freshly ground black pepper
serves 4

1 ▲ Wash the fennel bulbs and remove any brown or stringy outer leaves. Slice the bulbs and stems into thin pieces. Place in a shallow serving bowl.

2 ▲ Peel the oranges with a sharp knife, cutting away the white pith. Slice thinly. Cut each slice into thirds. Arrange over the fennel, adding any juice from the oranges.

3 ▲ For the dressing, mix the oil and lemon juice together. Season with salt and pepper. Pour the dressing over the salad. Mix well.

4 ▲ Slice the white and green sections of the scallions thinly. Sprinkle over the salad.

Potato Salad

Insalata di patate

This salad is dressed while the potatoes are still warm, so the flavors are fully absorbed. Use the best olive oil available.

Ingredients
2 lb waxy potatoes
For the dressing
6 tbsp extra-virgin olive oil
juice of 1 lemon
1 clove garlic, very finely chopped
2 tbsp chopped fresh herbs, such as
    parsley, basil, thyme or oregano
salt and freshly ground black pepper
serves 6

1 Wash the potatoes, but do not peel them. Boil or steam them until tender. When they are cool enough to handle, peel them. Cut the potatoes into dice.

2 ▲ While the potatoes are cooking, mix together all the dressing ingredients.

3 ▲ Pour the dressing over the potatoes while they are still warm. Mix well. Serve at room temperature or cold.

Chickpea Salad

Ceci in insalata

This salad makes a good light meal, and is quickly assembled if canned chickpeas are used.

Ingredients
2 × 14 oz cans chickpeas, or 2 cups
    cooked chickpeas
6 scallions, chopped
2 medium tomatoes, cut into cubes
1 small red onion, finely chopped
12 black olives, pitted and cut in half
1 tbsp capers, drained
2 tbsp finely chopped fresh parsley or
    mint leaves
4 hard-boiled eggs, cut into quarters, to
    garnish
For the dressing
5 tbsp olive oil
3 tbsp wine vinegar
salt and freshly ground black pepper
serves 4–6

1 Rinse the chickpeas under cold water. Drain. Place in a serving bowl.

2 ▲ Mix in the other vegetables with the olives, capers and parsley.

3 ▲ Mix the dressing ingredients together in a small cup.

4 ▲ Toss the salad with the mixed herbs. Pour the dressing over the salad and mix well. Taste for seasoning. Allow to stand for at least 1 hour. Just before serving decorate the salad with the egg wedges.

~ VARIATION ~

Other types of canned cooked beans may be substituted in this salad, such as cannellini or borlotti.

Tuscan Baked Beans

Fagioli al forno alla toscana

Beans, both dried and fresh, are particularly popular in Tuscany, where they are cooked in many different ways. In this vegetarian dish the beans are flavored with fresh sage leaves.

Ingredients

1 lb 6 oz dried beans, such as cannellini
4 tbsp olive oil
2 cloves garlic, crushed
3 leaves fresh sage (if fresh sage is not available use 4 tbsp chopped fresh parsley)
1 leek, finely sliced
1 × 14 oz can plum tomatoes, chopped, with their juice
salt and freshly ground black pepper
serves 6–8

3 ▲ In a large deep baking dish combine the beans with the leek and tomatoes. Stir in the oil with the garlic and sage. Add enough fresh water to cover the beans by 1 inch. Mix well. Cover the dish with a lid or foil, and place in the center of the preheated oven. Bake for 1¾ hours.

4 ▲ Remove the dish from the oven, stir the beans, and season with salt and pepper. Return the beans to the oven, uncovered, and cook for another 15 minutes, or until the beans are tender. Remove from the oven and allow to stand for 7–8 minutes before serving. Serve hot or at room temperature.

1 ▲ Carefully pick over the beans, discarding any stones or other particles. Place the beans in a large bowl and cover with water. Soak for at least 6 hours, or overnight. Drain.

2 ▲ Preheat the oven to 350°F. In a small saucepan heat the oil and sauté the garlic cloves and sage leaves for 3–4 minutes until garlic is tender but not brown. Remove from the heat.

Stewed Lentils

Lenticchie in umido

In Italy lentils are very often eaten as an accompaniment to duck and to zampone or cotechino sausages, but they are also good by themselves.

Ingredients

2 cups green or brown lentils
3 tbsp olive oil
¼ cup pancetta or salt pork
1 medium onion, very finely chopped
1 stalk celery, very finely sliced
1 carrot, very finely chopped
1 clove garlic
1 bay leaf
3 tbsp chopped fresh parsley
salt and freshly ground black pepper
serves 6

1 ▲ Carefully pick over the lentils, removing any pitts or other particles. Place them in a large bowl and cover with water. Soak for several hours. Drain.

3 ▲ Add the celery and carrot and cook for 3–4 minutes more.

2 ▲ In a large heavy saucepan heat the oil. Add the pancetta or salt pork and cook for 3 or 4 minutes. Stir in the onion, and cook over low heat until it is soft.

4 ▲ Add the lentils to the pan, stirring to coat them with the fat. Pour in enough boiling water just to cover the lentils. Stir well, adding the whole garlic clove, the bay leaf and the parsley. Season with salt and pepper. Cook over moderate heat until the lentils are tender, about 1 hour. Discard the garlic and bay leaf. Serve hot or at room temperature.

PASTA

Dried and home-made egg pastas are easy to prepare and the varied shapes are always family favourites. Nutritious fresh sauces made from vegetables, fish, meat and cheese offer endless possibilities for first and main courses.

How to Make Egg Pasta by Hand

This classic recipe for egg noodles from Emilia-Romagna calls for just three ingredients: flour and eggs, with a little salt. In other regions of Italy water, milk or oil are sometimes added. Use plain unbleached white flour, and large eggs. As a general guide, use ½ cup of flour to each egg Quantities will vary with the exact size of the eggs.

To serve 3–4
2 eggs, salt
1 cup flour

To serve 4–6
3 eggs, salt
1½ cups flour

To serve 6–8
4 eggs, salt
2 cups flour

1 ▲ Place the flour in the center of a clean smooth work surface. Make a well in the middle. Break the eggs into the well. Add a pinch of salt.

2 Start beating the eggs with a fork, gradually drawing the flour from the inside walls of the well. As the paste thickens, continue the mixing with your hands. Incorporate as much flour as possible until the mixture forms a mass. It will still be lumpy. If it still sticks to your hands, add a little more flour. Set the dough aside. Scrape off all traces of the dough from the work surface until it is perfectly smooth. Wash and dry your hands.

About Pasta

Most pasta is made from durum wheat flour and water – durum is a special kind of wheat with a very high protein content. Egg pasta, *pasta all'uova*, contains flour and eggs, and is used for flat noodles such as tagliatelle, or for lasagne. Very little whole wheat pasta is eaten in Italy, but it is quite popular in other countries.

All these types of pasta are available dried in packets, and will keep almost indefinitely. Fresh pasta is now more widely available and can be bought in most supermarkets. It can be very good, but can never compare to home-made egg pasta.

Pasta comes in countless shapes and sizes. It is very difficult to give a definite list, as the names for the shapes vary from country to country. In some cases, just within Italy, the same shape can appear with several different names, depending upon which region it is in. The pasta shapes called for in this book, as well as many others, are illustrated in the introduction. The most common names have been listed.

Most of the recipes in this book specify the pasta shape most appropriate for a particular sauce. They can, of course, be replaced with another kind. A general rule is that long pasta goes better with tomato or thinner sauces, while short pasta is best for chunkier, meatier sauces. But this rule should not be followed too rigidly. Part of the fun of cooking and eating pasta is in the endless combinations of sauce and pasta shapes.

3 ▲ Lightly flour the work surface. Knead the dough by pressing it away from you with the heel of your hands, and then folding it over towards you. Repeat this action over and over, turning the dough as you knead. Work for about 10 minutes, or until the dough is smooth and elastic.

4 ▲ If you are using more than 2 eggs, divide the dough in half. Flour the rolling pin and the work surface. Pat the dough into a disc and begin rolling it out into a flat circle, rotating it one quarter turn after each roll to keep its shape round. Roll until the disc is about ⅛ in thick.

5 ▲ Roll out the dough until it is paper-thin by rolling up onto the

rolling pin and simultaneously giving a sideways stretching with the hands. Wrap the near edge of the dough around the center of the rolling pin, and begin rolling the dough up away from you. As you roll back and forth, slide your hands from the center towards the outer edges of the pin, stretching and thinning out the pasta.

6 ▲ Quickly repeat these movements until about two-thirds of the sheet of pasta is wrapped around the pin. Lift and turn the wrapped pasta sheet about 45° before unrolling it. Repeat the rolling and stretching process, starting from a new point of the sheet each time to keep it evenly thin. By the end (this process should not last more than 8 to 10 minutes or the dough will lose its elasticity) the whole sheet should be smooth and almost transparent. If the dough is still sticky, lightly flour your hands as you continue rolling and stretching.

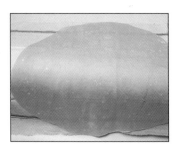

7 ▲ If you are making noodles (tagliatelle, fettuccine etc.) lay a clean dish towel on a table or other flat surface, and unroll the pasta sheet on it, letting about a third of the sheet hang over the edge of the table. Rotate

the dough every 10 minutes. Roll out the second sheet of dough if you are using more than 2 eggs. After 25–30 minutes the pasta will have dried enough to cut. Do not overdry or the pasta will crack as it is cut.

8 ▲ To cut tagliatelle, fettuccine or tagliolini, fold the sheet of pasta into a flat roll about 4 in wide. Cut across the roll to form noodles of the desired width. Tagliolini is ⅛ in; Fettuccine is ⅙ in; Tagliatelle is ¼ in. After cutting, open out the noodles, and let them dry for about 5 minutes before cooking. These noodles may be stored for some weeks without refrigeration. Allow them to dry completely before storing them, uncovered, in a dry cupboard.

9 ▲ To cut the pasta for lasagne or pappardelle, do not fold or dry the rolled out dough. Lasagne is made by cutting rectangles approximately 5 in by 3½ in. Pappardelle are large noodles cut with a fluted pastry wheel. They are about ¾ in wide.

Egg Pasta Made by Machine

Making pasta with a machine is quick and easy. The results are perhaps not quite as fine as with handmade pasta, but they are certainly better than store-bought pastas.

You will need a pasta-making machine, either hand-cranked or electric. Use the same proportions of eggs, flours and salt as for Handmade Egg Pasta.

orange. Place the remaining dough between two soup plates. Feed the dough through the rollers. Fold it in half, end to end, and feed it through again 7 or 8 times, turning it and folding it over after each kneading. The dough should be smooth and fairly evenly rectangular. If it sticks to the machine, brush with flour. Lay it out on a lightly floured work surface or on a clean dish towel, and repeat with the remaining dough, broken into pieces the same size.

1 ▲ Place the flour in the center of a clean smooth work surface. Make a well in the middle. Break the eggs into the well. Add a pinch of salt. Start beating the eggs with a fork, gradually drawing the flour from the inside walls of the well. As the paste thickens, continue mixing with your hands. Incorporate as much flour as possible until the mixture forms a mass. It will still be lumpy. If it sticks to your hands, add a little more flour. Set the dough aside and scrape the work surface clean.

3 ▲ Adjust the machine to the next line setting. Feed each strip through once only, and replace on the drying surface. Keep them in the order in which they were first kneaded.

4 ▲ Reset the machine to the next setting. Repeat, passing each strip through once. Repeat for each remaining roller setting until the pasta is the right thickness – for most purposes this is given by the next to last setting, except for very delicate strips such as tagliolini, or for ravioli. If the pasta strips get too long, cut them in half to facilitate handling.

5 ▲ When all the strips are the desired thickness they may be machine-cut into noodles, or hand-cut for lasagne or pappardelle, as described for handmade pasta earlier. When making noodles, be sure the pasta is fairly dry, but not brittle, or the noodles may stick togther when cut. Select the desired width of cutter, and feed the strips through.

6 Separate the noodles, and leave to dry for at least 15 minutes before using. They may be stored for some weeks without refrigeration. Allow them to dry completely before storing them, uncovered, in a dry cupboard. They may also be frozen, first loose on trays and then packed together.

7 If you are making stuffed pasta (ravioli, cannelloni etc.) do not let the pasta strips dry out before filling them, but proceed immediately with the individual recipes.

2 ▲ Set the machine rollers at their widest (kneading) setting. Pull off a piece of dough the size of a small

~ PASTA VERDE ~

Follow the same recipe, adding ¼ cup cooked, very finely chopped spinach after having been squeezed very dry) to the eggs and flour. You may have to add a little more flour to absorb the moisture from the spinach. This pasta is very suitable for stuffed recipes, as it seals better than plain egg pasta.

How to Cook Dried Pasta

Store-bought and home-made pasta are cooked in the same way, though the timings vary greatly. Home-made pasta cooks virtually in the time it takes for the water to return to a boil after it is put in.

1 Always cook pasta in a large pot with a generous amount of rapidly boiling water. Use at least 5 cups of water to each ½ cup pasta.

2 ▲ The water should be salted at least 2 minutes before the pasta is added, to give the salt time to dissolve. Add about 1½ tbsp salt per 2 cups of pasta. You may want to vary the saltiness of the cooking water.

3 ▲ Drop the pasta into the boiling water all at once. Use a wooden spoon to help ease long pasta in as it softens, to prevent it from breaking. Stir frequently to prevent the pasta sticking to itself or to the pan. Cook the pasta at a fast boil, but be prepared to lower the heat if it boils over.

4 Timing is critical in pasta cooking. Follow package indications for store-bought pasta, but it is best in all cases to test for doneness by tasting, several times if necessary. In Italy pasta is always eaten *al dente*, which mens firm to the bite. Cooked this way it is just tender, but its "soul" (the innermost part) is still firm.

5 ▲ Place a colander in the sink before the pasta has finished cooking. As soon as the pasta tastes done, tip it all into the colander (you may first want to reserve a cupful of the hot cooking water to add to the sauce if it needs thinning). Shake the colander lightly to remove most but not all of the cooking water. Pasta should never be over-drained.

6 ▲ Quickly turn the pasta into a warmed serving dish, and immediately toss it with a little butter or oil, or the prepared sauce. Alternatively, turn it into the cooking pan with the sauce, where it will be cooked for 1–2 minutes more as it is mixed into the sauce. Never allow pasta to sit undressed, as it will stick together and become unpalatable.

How to Cook Egg Pasta

Fresh egg pasta, especially home-made, cooks very much faster than dried pasta. Make sure everything is ready (the sauce, serving dishes, etc.) before you start boiling egg pasta, as there will not be time once the cooking starts, and egg pasta becomes soft and mushy very quickly.

1 Always cook pasta in a large pot with a generous amount of rapidly boiling water. Use at least 5 cups of water to a quantity of pasta made with 1 cup of flour. Salt the water as for dried pasta.

2 ▲ Drop the pasta into the boiling water all at once. Stir gently to prevent the pasta sticking to itself or to the pan. Cook the pasta at a fast boil.

3 ▲ Freshly made pasta can be done as little as 15 seconds after their cooking water comes back to a boil. Stuffed pasta takes a few minutes longer. When done, tip the pasta into the colander and proceed as for dried pasta.

Basic Tomato Sauce

Sugo di pomodoro alla napoletana

Tomato sauce is without a doubt the most popular dressing for pasta in Italy. This sauce is best made with fresh tomatoes, but works well with canned plum tomatoes.

Ingredients
4 tbsp olive oil
1 medium onion, very finely chopped
1 clove garlic, finely chopped
1 lb tomatoes, fresh or canned, chopped,
    with their juice
salt and freshly ground black pepper
a few leaves fresh basil or sprigs parsley
for 4 servings of pasta

1 Heat the oil in a medium saucepan. Add the onion, and cook over moderate heat until it is translucent, 5–8 minutes.

2 ▲ Stir in the garlic and the tomatoes with their juice (add 3 tbsp of water if you are using fresh tomatoes). Season with salt and pepper. Add the herbs. Cook for 20–30 minutes.

3 ▲ Pass the sauce through a food mill or purée in a food processor. To serve, reheat gently, correct the seasoning and pour over the drained pasta.

Special Tomato Sauce

Sugo di pomodoro

The tomatoes in this sauce are enhanced by the addition of extra vegetables. It is good served with all types of pasta or could be served as an accompaniment to stuffed vegetables.

Ingredients
1⅔ lb tomatoes, fresh or canned,
    chopped
1 carrot, chopped
1 stalk celery, chopped
1 medium onion, chopped
1 clove garlic, crushed
5 tbsp olive oil
salt and freshly ground black pepper
a few leaves fresh basil or a small pinch
    dried oregano
for 6 servings of pasta

1 Place all the ingredients in a medium heavy saucepan, and simmer together for 30 minutes.

2 ▲ Purée the sauce in a food processor, or press through a sieve.

3 ▲ Return the sauce to the pan, correct the seasoning, and simmer again for about 15 minutes.

~ COOK'S TIP ~

This sauce may be spooned into freezer bags and frozen until required. Allow to thaw to room temperature before re-heating.

Linguine with Pesto Sauce

Linguine con pesto

Pesto originates in Liguria, where the sea breezes are said to give the local basil a particularly fine flavor. It is traditionally made with a mortar and pestle, but it is easier to make in a food processor or blender. Freeze any spare pesto in an ice cube tray.

Ingredients

¾ cup fresh basil leaves
3–4 cloves garlic, peeled
3 tbsp pine nuts
½ tsp salt
5 tbsp olive oil
½ cup freshly grated Parmesan cheese
4 tbsp freshly grated pecorino cheese
freshly ground black pepper
1¼ lb linguine

serves 5–6

1 ▲ Place the basil, garlic, pine nuts, salt and olive oil in a blender or food processor and process until smooth. Remove to a bowl. (If desired, the sauce may be frozen at this point, before the cheeses are added).

2 ▲ Stir in the cheeses (use all Parmesan if pecorino is not available). Taste for seasoning.

3 ▲ Cook the pasta in a large pan of rapidly boiling salted water until it is *al dente.* Just before draining it, take about 4 tbsp of the cooking water and stir it into the sauce.

4 Drain the pasta and toss with the sauce. Serve immediately.

Bolognese Meat Sauce

Ragù alla bolognese

This great meat sauce is a speciality of Bologna. It is delicious with tagliatelle or short pastas such as penne or conchiglie as well as spaghetti, and is indispensable in baked lasagne. It keeps well in the refrigerator for several days and can also be frozen.

Ingredients

2 tbsp butter
4 tbsp olive oil
1 medium onion, finely chopped
2 tbsp pancetta or unsmoked bacon,
    finely chopped
1 carrot, finely sliced
1 stalk celery, finely sliced
1 clove garlic, finely chopped
12 oz lean ground beef
salt and freshly ground black pepper
⅔ cup red wine
½ cup milk
1 × 14 oz can plum tomatoes, chopped,
    with their juice
1 bay leaf
¼ tsp fresh thyme leaves
for 6 servings of pasta

3 ▲ Pour in the wine, raise the heat slightly, and cook until the liquid evaporates, 3–4 minutes. Add the milk, and cook until it evaporates.

4 ▲ Stir in the tomatoes with their juice, and the herbs. Bring the sauce to a boil. Reduce the heat to low, and simmer, uncovered for 1½–2 hours, stirring occasionally. Correct the seasoning before serving.

1 ▲ Heat the butter and oil in a heavy saucepan or earthenware pot. Add the onion, and cook over moderate heat for 3–4 minutes. Add the pancetta, and cook until the onion is translucent. Stir in the carrot, celery and garlic. Cook 3–4 minutes more.

2 Add the beef, and crumble it into the vegetables with a fork. Stir until the meat loses its red color. Season with salt and pepper.

Spaghetti with Garlic and Oil

Spaghetti con aglio e olio

This is one of the simplest and most satisfying pasta dishes of all. It is very popular throughout Italy. Use the best quality oil available for this dish.

Ingredients
1 lb spaghetti
6 tbsp extra-virgin olive oil
3 cloves garlic, chopped
4 tbsp chopped fresh parsley
salt and freshly ground black pepper
freshly grated Parmesan cheese, to serve
    (optional)
serves 4

1 Drop the spaghetti into a large pan of rapidly boiling salted water.

2 ▲ In a large frying pan heat the oil and gently sauté the garlic until it is barely golden. Do not let it brown or it will taste bitter. Stir in the parsley. Season with salt and pepper. Remove from the heat until the pasta is ready.

3 ▲ Drain the pasta when it is barely *al dente*. Tip it into the pan with the oil and garlic, and cook together for 2–3 minutes, stirring well to coat the spaghetti with the sauce. Serve at once in a warmed serving bowl, with Parmesan, if desired.

Spaghetti with Walnut Sauce

Spaghetti con salsa di noci

Like pesto, this sauce is traditionally ground in a mortar and pestle, but works just as well made in a food processor. It is also very good on tagliatelle and other noodles.

Ingredients
1 cup walnut pieces or halves
3 tbsp plain breadcrumbs
3 tbsp olive or walnut oil
3 tbsp chopped fresh parsley
1–2 cloves garlic (optional)
¼ cup butter, at room temperature
2 tbsp cream
salt and freshly ground black pepper
14 oz whole wheat spaghetti
freshly grated Parmesan cheese, to serve
serves 4

1 Drop the nuts into a small pan of boiling water, and cook for 1–2 minutes. Drain. Slip off the skins. Dry on paper towels. Coarsely chop and set aside about a quarter of the nuts.

2 ▲ Place the remaining nuts, the breadcrumbs, oil, parsley and garlic, if using, in a food processor or blender. Process to a paste. Remove to a bowl, and stir in the softened butter and the cream. Season with salt and pepper.

3 ▲ Cook the pasta in a large pan of rapidly boiling salted water until *al dente*. Drain, and toss with the sauce. Sprinkle with the reserved chopped nuts, and pass the Parmesan separately.

Fusilli with Peppers and Onions

Fusilli con peperoni

Peppers are characteristic of southern Italy. When broiled and peeled they have a delicious smoky flavor, and are easier to digest.

Ingredients

1 lb red and yellow peppers
    (about 2 large ones)
6 tbsp olive oil
1 large red onion, thinly sliced
2 cloves garlic, minced
1 lb fusilli or other short pasta
salt and freshly ground black pepper
3 tbsp finely chopped fresh parsley
freshly grated Parmesan cheese, to serve
serves 4

1 ▲ Place the peppers under a hot broiler and turn occasionally until they are black and blistered on all sides. Remove from the heat, place in a paper bag and leave for 5 minutes.

2 ▲ Peel the peppers. Cut them into quarters, remove the stems and seeds, and slice into thin strips. Bring a large pan of water to a boil.

3 ▲ Heat the oil in a large frying pan. Add the onion, and cook over moderate heat until it is translucent, 5–8 minutes. Stir in the garlic, and cook for 2 minutes more.

4 ▲ Add salt and the pasta to the boiling water, and cook until the pasta is just *al dente*.

~ COOK'S TIP ~

Peppers belong to the *capsicum annum* family. They were brought to Europe by Columbus who discovered them in Haiti. The large red, yellow and orange peppers are usually sweeter than the green varieties, and have a fuller flavor.

5 ▲ Meanwhile, add the peppers to the onions, and mix together gently. Stir in about 3 tbsp of the pasta cooking water. Season with salt and pepper. Stir in the parsley.

6 ▲ Drain the pasta. Tip it into the frying pan with the vegetables, and cook over moderate heat for 1–2 minutes, stirring constantly to mix the pasta into the sauce. Serve with the Parmesan passed separately.

Orecchiette with Broccoli

Pasta e broccoli

Puglia, in southern Italy, specializes in imaginative pasta and vegetable combinations. Using the broccoli cooking water for boiling the pasta gives it more of the vegetable's flavor.

Ingredients

1¾ lb broccoli
1 lb orecchiette or penne
6 tbsp olive oil
3 cloves garlic, finely chopped
6 anchovy fillets in oil
salt and freshly ground black pepper
serves 6

1 Peel the stems of the broccoli, starting from the base and pulling up towards the florets with a knife. Discard the woody parts of the stem. Cut florets and stems into 2 in pieces.

2 ▲ Bring a large pan of water to a boil. Drop in the broccoli, and boil until barely tender, about 5–8 minutes. Remove the broccoli pieces from the pan to a serving bowl. Do not discard the cooking water.

3 ▲ Add salt to the broccoli cooking water. Bring it back to a boil. Drop in the pasta, stir well, and cook until it is *al dente*.

4 ▲ While the pasta is boiling, heat the oil in a small frying pan. Add the garlic and, after 2–3 minutes, the anchovy fillets. Using a fork, mash the anchovies and garlic to a paste. Cook for 3–4 minutes more.

5 ▲ Before draining the pasta, ladle 1–2 cupfuls of the cooking water over the broccoli. Add the drained pasta and the hot anchovy and oil mixture. Mix well, and season with salt and pepper if necessary. Serve at once.

Spaghetti with Eggs and Bacon

Spaghetti alla carbonara

One of the classic pasta sauces, about which a debate remains: whether or not it should contain cream. Purists believe that it should not.

Ingredients

2 tbsp olive oil
generous ½ cup bacon, cut into
    matchsticks
1 clove garlic, crushed
1 lb spaghetti
3 eggs, at room temperature
¾ cup freshly grated Parmesan cheese
salt and freshly ground black pepper
serves 4

3 ▲ While the pasta is cooking, warm a large serving bowl and break the eggs into it. Beat in the Parmesan cheese with a fork, and season with salt and pepper.

4 ▲ As soon as the pasta is done, drain it quickly, and mix it into the egg mixture. Pour on the hot bacon and its fat. Stir well. The heat from the pasta and bacon fat will cook the eggs. Serve immediately.

1 ▲ Bring a large pan of water to a boil. In a medium frying pan, heat the oil and sauté the bacon and the garlic until the bacon renders its fat and starts to brown. Remove and discard the garlic. Keep the bacon and its fat hot until needed.

2 ▲ Add salt and the spaghetti to the boiling water, and cook until it is *al dente*.

Short Pasta with Cauliflower

Pennoni rigati con cavolfiore

This is a pasta version of cauliflower cheese. The cauliflower water is used to boil the pasta.

Ingredients
1 medium cauliflower
2 cups milk
1 bay leaf
¼ cup butter
½ cup flour
salt and freshly ground black pepper
¾ cup freshly grated Parmesan or
    Romano cheese
1¼ lb pennoni rigati, tortiglioni, or other
    short pasta
serves 6

1 Bring a large pan of water to a boil. Wash the cauliflower well, and separate it into florets. Boil the florets until they are just tender, about 8–10 minutes. Remove them from the pan with a strainer or slotted spoon. Chop the cauliflower into bite-size pieces and set aside. Do not discard the cooking water.

2 ▲ Make a béchamel sauce by gently heating the milk with the bay leaf in a small saucepan. Do not let it boil. Melt the butter in a medium heavy saucepan. Add the flour, and mix it in well with a wire whisk ensuring there are no lumps. Cook for 2–3 minutes, but do not let the butter burn.

3 Strain the hot milk into the flour and butter mixture all at once, and mix smoothly with the whisk.

4 Bring the sauce to a boil, stirring constantly, and cook for 4–5 minutes more. Season with salt and pepper. Add the cheese, and stir over low heat until it melts. Stir in the cauliflower.

5 ▲ Bring the cooking water back to a boil. Add salt, and stir in the pasta. Cook until it is *al dente*. Drain, and tip the pasta into a warm serving bowl. Pour over the sauce. Mix well, and serve at once.

Spaghetti with Bacon and Onion

Spaghetti all'amatriciana

This easy sauce is quickly made from ingredients that are almost always at hand.

Ingredients
2 tbsp olive oil
½ cup unsmoked lean bacon, cut into
    matchsticks
1 small onion, finely chopped
½ cup dry white wine
1 lb tomatoes, fresh or canned, chopped
¼ tsp thyme leaves
salt and freshly ground black pepper
1¼ lb spaghetti
freshly grated Parmesan cheese, to serve
serves 6

1 In a medium frying pan, heat the oil. Add the bacon and onion, and cook over low to moderate heat until the onion is golden and the bacon has rendered its fat and is beginning to brown, about 8–10 minutes. Bring a large pan of water to a boil.

2 ▲ Add the wine to the bacon and onion, raise the heat, and cook rapidly until the liquid boils off. Add the tomatoes, thyme, salt and pepper. Cover, and cook over moderate heat for 10–15 minutes.

3 ▲ Meanwhile, add salt to the boiling water, and cook the pasta until it is *al dente*. Drain, toss with the sauce, and serve with the grated Parmesan.

Spaghetti with Olives and Capers   *Spaghetti alla puttanesca*

This spicy sauce originated in the Naples area, where it was named for the local women of easy virtue. It can be quickly assembled using a few kitchen cupboard staples.

Ingredients
4 tbsp olive oil
2 cloves garlic, finely chopped
small piece of dried chili, crumbled
1 × 2 oz can of anchovy fillets, chopped
12 oz tomatoes, fresh or canned,
    chopped
⅔ cup pitted black olives
2 tbsp capers, rinsed
1 tbsp tomato paste
1 lb spaghetti
2 tbsp chopped fresh parsley, to serve
serves 4

3 ▲ Add the tomatoes, olives, capers and tomato paste. Stir well and cook over moderate heat.

4 Add salt to the boiling water, and put in the spaghetti. Stir, and cook until the pasta is just *al dente*. Drain.

5 ▲ Turn the spaghetti into the sauce. Raise the heat, and cook for 1–2 minutes, turning the pasta constantly. Sprinkle with parsley if desired and serve. Traditionally, no cheese is served with this sauce.

1 ▲ Bring a large pan of water to a boil. Heat the oil in a large frying pan. Add the garlic and the dried chili, and cook for 2–3 minutes until the garlic is just golden.

2 ▲ Add the anchovies, and mash them into the garlic with a fork.

Linguine with Clam and Tomato Sauce *Linguine con vongole*

There are two types of traditional Italian clam sauce for pasta: one with and one without

tomatoes. This tomato version can be made with canned clams if fresh are not available.

Ingredients

2 lb fresh clams in their shells, or 12 oz
    canned clams, with their liquid
6 tbsp olive oil
1 clove garlic, crushed
14 oz tomatoes, fresh or canned, very
    finely chopped
1 lb linguine
4 tbsp chopped fresh parsley
salt and freshly ground black pepper
serves 4

1 ▲ Scrub and rinse the clams well
under cold running water. Place them
in a large saucepan with a cupful of
water, and heat until the clams begin
to open. Lift each clam out as soon as it
opens, and scoop it out of its shell
using a small spoon. Place in a bowl.

2 If the clams are large, chop them
into 2 or 3 pieces. Reserve any liquids
from the shells in a separate bowl.
When all the clams have opened
(discard any that do not open) pour
the cooking liquids into the juices
from the clams, and strain them
through a piece of paper towel to
remove any sand. If using canned
clams, use the liquid from the can.

3 Bring a large pot of water to a boil
for the pasta. Place the olive oil in a
medium saucepan with the garlic.
Cook over moderate heat until the
garlic is just golden.

4 ▲ Remove the garlic and discard.
Add the chopped tomatoes to the oil,
and pour in the clam liquid. Mix well
and cook over low to moderate heat
until the sauce begins to dry out and
thicken slightly. Add salt and the pasta
to the boiling water.

5 ▲ A minute or two before the pasta
is ready to be drained, stir the parsley
and the clams into the tomato sauce,
and raise the heat. Add some freshly
ground black pepper, and taste for
seasoning. Drain the pasta, and turn it
into a serving bowl. Pour on the hot
sauce, and mix well before serving.

Spaghetti with Mussels

Spaghetti con cozze

Mussels are popular in all the coastal regions of Italy, and are delicious with pasta. This simple dish is greatly improved by using the freshest mussels available.

Ingredients

2 lb fresh mussels, in their shells
5 tbsp olive oil
3 cloves garlic, finely chopped
4 tbsp finely chopped fresh parsley
4 tbsp white wine
1 lb spaghetti
salt and freshly ground black pepper
serves 4

1 ▲ Scrub the mussels well under cold running water, cutting off the "beard" with a small sharp knife.

2 ▲ Bring a large pan of water to a boil for the pasta. Place the mussels with a cupful of water in another large saucepan over moderate heat. As soon as they open, lift them out one by one.

3 ▲ When all the mussels have opened (discard any that do not), strain the liquid in the saucepan through a layer of paper towels and reserve until needed.

4 ▲ Heat the oil in a large frying pan. Add the garlic and parsley, and cook for 2–3 minutes. Add the mussels, their strained juices and the wine. Cook over moderate heat. Meanwhile add salt to the boiling water, and drop in the pasta.

5 ▲ Add a generous amount of freshly ground black pepper to the sauce. Taste for seasoning, adding salt as necessary.

6 ▲ Drain the pasta when it is *al dente*. Tip it into the frying pan with the sauce, and stir well over moderate heat for 1–2 minutes more. Serve at once, without cheese.

~ COOK'S TIP ~

Mussels should be firmly closed when fresh. If a mussel is slightly open, pinch it closed. If it remains closed on its own, it is alive. If it remains open, discard it. Fresh mussels should be consumed as soon as possible after being purchased. They may be kept in a bowl of cold water in the refrigerator.

Pasta with Fresh Sardine Sauce

Pasta con sarde

In this classic Sicilian dish, fresh sardines are combined with raisins and pine nuts.

Ingredients
3 tbsp sultanas
1 lb fresh sardines
6 tbsp breadcrumbs
1 small fennel bulb
6 tbsp olive oil
1 medium onion, very thinly sliced
3 tbsp pine nuts
½ tsp fennel seeds
salt and freshly ground black pepper
1 lb long hollow pasta such as percatelli,
    ziti, or bucatini
serves 4

1 Soak the sultanas in warm water for 15 minutes. Drain and pat dry.

2 ▲ Clean the sardines. Open each one out flat and remove the back bone and head. Wash well and shake dry. Sprinkle with breadcrumbs.

3 ▲ Coarsely chop the top fronds of fennel and reserve. Pull off a few outer leaves and wash. Fill a large pan with enough water to cook the pasta. Add the fennel leaves and bring to a boil.

4 ▲ Heat the oil in a large frying pan and sauté the onion lightly until soft. Remove to a side dish. Add the sardines, a few at a time, and cook over moderate heat until golden on both sides, turning them once carefully. When all the sardines have been cooked, gently return them to the pan. Add the onion, and the sultanas, pine nuts and fennel seeds. Season with salt and pepper.

5 ▲ Take about 4 tbsp of the boiling water for the pasta, and add it to the sauce. Add salt to the boiling water, and drop in the pasta. Cook until it is *al dente*. Drain, and remove the fennel leaves. Dress the pasta with the sauce. Divide between individual serving plates, arranging several sardines on each. Sprinkle with the reserved chopped fennel tops before serving.

Baked Macaroni with Cheese   *Maccheroni gratinati al forno*

This delicious dish is perhaps less common in Italy than other pasta dishes, but has become a family favorite around the world.

Ingredients
2 cups milk
1 bay leaf
3 blades mace, or pinch of grated nutmeg
4 tbsp butter
⅓ cup flour
salt and freshly ground black pepper
1½ cups grated Parmesan or Cheddar
    cheese, or a combination of both
⅓ cup breadcrumbs
1 lb macaroni or other short hollow pasta
serves 6

1 Make a béchamel sauce by gently heating the milk with the bay leaf and mace in a small saucepan. Do not let it boil. Melt the butter in a medium heavy saucepan. Add the flour, and mix it in well with a wire whisk. Cook for 2–3 minutes, but do not let the butter burn. Strain the hot milk into the flour and butter mixture all at once, and mix smoothly with the whisk. Bring the sauce to a boil, stirring constantly, and cook for 4–5 minutes more.

3 ▲ Bring a large pan of water to a boil. Preheat the oven to 400°F. Grease an ovenproof dish, and sprinkle with some breadcrumbs. Add salt and the pasta to the boiling water, and cook until it is barely *al dente*. Do not overcook, as the pasta will get a second cooking in the oven.

4 ▲ Drain the pasta, and combine it with the sauce. Pour it into the prepared ovenproof dish. Sprinkle the top with the remaining breadcrumbs and grated cheese, and place in the center of the preheated oven. Bake for 20 minutes.

2 ▲ Season with salt and pepper, and the nutmeg if no mace has been used. Add all but 2 tbsp of the cheese, and stir over low heat until it melts. Place a layer of plastic wrap right on the surface of the sauce to stop a skin from forming, and set aside.

Penne with Tuna and Mozzarella   *Penne con tonno e mozzarella*

This tasty sauce is quickly made from kitchen cupboard staples, with the addition of fresh mozzarella. If possible, use tuna canned in olive oil.

Ingredients

1 lb penne, or other short pasta
1 tbsp capers, in brine or salt
2 cloves garlic
3 tbsp chopped fresh parsley
1 × 7 oz can of tuna, drained
5 tbsp olive oil
salt and freshly ground black pepper
⅔ cup mozzarella cheese, cut into
    small dice
serves 4

1 Bring a large pan of salted water to a boil and drop in the pasta.

2 ▲ Rinse the capers well in water. Chop them finely with the garlic. Combine with the parsley and the tuna. Stir in the oil, and season with salt and pepper, if necessary.

3 ▲ Drain the pasta when it is just *al dente*. Tip it into a large frying pan. Add the tuna sauce and the diced mozzarella, and cook over moderate heat, stirring constantly, until the cheese just begins to melt. Serve at once.

Spaghettini with Vodka and Caviar   *Spaghettini con vodka e caviale*

This is an elegant yet easy way to serve spaghettini. In Rome it is an after-theater favorite.

Ingredients

4 tbsp olive oil
3 scallions, thinly sliced
1 clove garlic, finely chopped
½ cup vodka
⅔ cup heavy cream
½ cup black or red caviar
salt and freshly ground black pepper
1 lb spaghettini
serves 4

1 ▲ Heat the oil in a small frying pan. Add the scallions and garlic, and cook gently for 4–5 minutes.

2 ▲ Add the vodka and cream, and cook over low heat for about 5–8 minutes more.

~ COOK'S TIP ~

The finest caviar is salted sturgeon roe. Red "caviar" is salmon roe, cheaper and often saltier than sturgeon roe, as is the black-dyed lump fish roe.

3 ▲ Remove from the heat and stir in the caviar. Season with salt and pepper as necessary.

4 Meanwhile, cook the spaghettini in a large pan of rapidly boiling salted water until *al dente*. Drain the pasta, and toss immediately with the sauce.

Pasta Bows with Shrimp and Peas   *Farfalle con gamberetti e piselli*

A small amount of saffron in the sauce gives this dish a lovely golden color.

Ingredients
3 tbsp olive oil
2 tbsp butter
2 scallions, chopped
12 oz fresh or frozen peeled shrimp
1¼ cups frozen petit pois or peas,
    thawed
1 lb farfalle
1 cup dry white wine
a few strands fresh saffron or ⅛ tsp
    powdered saffron
salt and freshly ground black pepper
2 tbsp chopped fresh fennel or dill,
    to serve
serves 4

1 Bring a large pan of water to a boil. Heat the oil and butter in a large frying pan and sauté the scallions lightly. Add the peas, and cook for 2–3 minutes.

2 ▲ Add salt and the pasta to the boiling water. Stir the wine and saffron into the peas. Raise the heat and cook until the wine is reduced by about half. Add the shrimp, and salt and pepper to taste. Cover the pan and reduce the heat to low.

3 ▲ Drain the pasta when it is *al dente*. Add it to the pan with the sauce. Stir over high heat for 1–2 minutes, coating the pasta with the sauce. Sprinkle with the fresh herbs, and serve at once.

Short Pasta with Spring Vegetables   *Pasta primavera*

This colorful sauce makes the most of new crops of fresh tender spring vegetables.

Ingredients
1 or 2 small young carrots
2 scallions
1 cup zucchini
2 tomatoes
½ cup shelled peas, fresh or frozen
½ cup green beans
1 yellow pepper
4 tbsp olive oil
2 tbsp butter
1 clove garlic, finely chopped
5–6 leaves fresh basil, torn into pieces
salt and freshly ground black pepper
1¼ lb short colored or plain pasta such as
    fusilli, penne or farfalle
freshly grated Parmesan cheese, to serve
serves 6

1 Cut all the vegetables into small, bite-size pieces.

2 ▲ Heat the oil and butter in a large frying pan. Add the chopped vegetables, and cook over moderate heat for 5–6 minutes, stirring occasionally. Add the garlic and the basil, and season with salt and pepper. Cover the pan, and cook for 5–8 minutes more, or until the vegetables are just tender.

3 ▲ Meanwhile, cook the pasta in a large pan of rapidly boiling salted water until *al dente*. Before draining it, reserve a cupful of the pasta water.

4 Turn the pasta into the pan with the sauce, and mix well to distribute the vegetables. If the sauce seems too dry, add a few tablespoons of the reserved pasta water. Serve with the Parmesan passed separately.

Baked Seafood Spaghetti

Spaghetti cartoccio

In this dish, each portion is baked and served in an individual packet which is then opened at the table. Use parchment paper or aluminium foil to make the packets.

Ingredients

1 lb fresh mussels
½ cup dry white wine
4 tbsp olive oil
2 cloves garlic, finely chopped
1 lb tomatoes, fresh or canned, peeled
    and finely chopped
1 lb spaghetti or other long pasta
2 tbsp chopped fresh parsley
8 oz peeled and deveined shrimp, fresh or
    frozen
salt and freshly ground black pepper
serves 4

1 ▲ Scrub the mussels well under cold running water, cutting off the "beard" with a small sharp knife. Place the mussels and the wine in a large saucepan and heat until they open.

2 ▲ Lift out the mussels and remove to a side dish. (Discard any that do not open.) Strain the cooking liquid through paper towels, and reserve until needed. Preheat the oven to 300°F.

3 ▲ Bring a large pan of water to a boil. In a medium saucepan, heat the oil and garlic together for 1–2 minutes. Add the tomatoes, and cook over moderate to high heat until they soften. Stir in ¾ cup of the cooking liquid from the mussels. Add salt and the pasta to the boiling water, and cook until it is just *al dente*.

4 ▲ Just before draining the pasta, add the parsley to the tomato sauce. Cook for 2 minutes. Taste for seasoning, adding salt and pepper as desired. Remove from the heat.

~ VARIATION ~

Canned mussels or clams may be substituted for fresh shellfish in this recipe. Add them to the tomato sauce with the shrimp.

5 ▲ Prepare 4 pieces of parchment paper or foil approximately 12 in × 18 in. Place each sheet in the center of a shallow bowl. Turn the drained pasta into a mixing bowl. Add the tomato sauce and mix well. Stir in the mussels and shrimp.

6 ▲ Divide the pasta and seafood between the four pieces of paper, placing a mound in the center of each, and twisting the paper ends together to make a closed packet. (The bowl under the paper will stop the sauce from spilling while the paper parcels are being closed.) Arrange on a large cookie sheet, and place in the center of the preheated oven. Bake for 8–10 minutes. Place one unopened packet on each individual serving plate.

Tuna Pasta Salad

Insalata di pasta con tonno

This easy pasta salad uses canned beans and tuna for a quick main dish.

Ingredients

1 lb short pasta, such as ruote, macaroni
  or farfalle
4 tbsp olive oil
2 × 7 oz cans tuna, drained
2 × 14 oz cans cannellini or borlotti
  beans, rinsed and drained
1 small red onion
2 stalks celery
juice of 1 lemon
2 tbsp chopped fresh parsley
salt and freshly ground black pepper
serves 6–8

1 Cook the pasta in a large pan of
rapidly boiling salted water until it is
al dente. Drain, and rinse under cold
water to stop cooking. Drain well and
turn into a large bowl. Toss with the
olive oil, and set aside. Allow to cool
completely before mixing with the
other ingredients.

2 ▲ Mix the flaked tuna and the beans
into the cooked pasta. Slice the onion
and celery very thinly and add them to
the pasta.

3 ▲ Combine the lemon juice with
the parsley. Mix into the other
ingredients. Season with salt and
pepper. Allow the salad to stand for at
least 1 hour before serving.

Chicken Pasta Salad

Insalata di pasta con pollo

This salad uses leftover chicken from a roast, or a cold poached chicken breast.

Ingredients

12 oz short pasta, such as mezze rigatoni,
  fusilli or penne
3 tbsp olive oil
1½ cups cold cooked chicken
2 small red and yellow peppers
  (about 7 oz)
⅓ cup pitted green olives
4 scallions, chopped
3 tbsp mayonnaise
1 tsp Worcestershire sauce
1 tbsp wine vinegar
salt and freshly ground black pepper
a few leaves fresh basil, to garnish
serves 4

1 Cook the pasta in a large pan of
rapidly boiling salted water until it is
al dente. Drain, and rinse under cold
water to stop the cooking. Drain well
and turn into a large bowl. Toss with
the olive oil, and set aside. Allow to
cool completely.

2 ▲ Cut the chicken into bite-size
pieces, removing any bones. Cut the
peppers into small pieces, removing
the seeds and stems.

3 ▲ Combine all the ingredients
except the pasta in a medium bowl.
Taste for seasoning, then mix into the
pasta. Garnish with the basil, and
serve chilled.

Whole Wheat Pasta Salad

Insalata di pasta integrale

This substantial vegetarian salad is easily assembled from any combination of seasonal vegetables. Use raw or lightly blanched vegetables, or a mixture of both.

Ingredients
1 lb short whole wheat pasta, such as
    fusilli or penne
3 tbsp olive oil
2 medium carrots
1 small bunch broccoli
1 cup shelled peas, fresh or frozen
1 red or yellow pepper
2 stalks celery
4 scallions
1 large tomato
½ cup pitted olives
For the dressing
3 tbsp wine or balsamic vinegar
4 tbsp olive oil
1 tbsp Dijon style mustard
1 tbsp sesame seeds
2 tsp finely chopped mixed fresh herbs,
    such as parsley, thyme and basil
salt and freshly ground black pepper
⅔ cup diced Cheddar or mozzarella, or a
    combination of both
serves 8

1 Cook the pasta in a large pan of rapidly boiling salted water until it is *al dente*. Drain, and rinse under cold water to stop the cooking. Drain well and turn into a large bowl. Toss with 3 tbsp of the olive oil, and set aside. Allow to cool completely before mixing with the other ingredients.

2 ▲ Lightly blanch the carrots, broccoli and peas in a large pan of boiling water. Refresh under cold water. Drain well.

3 ▲ Chop the carrots and broccoli into bite-size pieces and add to the pasta with the peas. Slice the pepper, celery, scallions and tomato into small pieces. Add them to the salad with the olives.

4 ▲ Make the dressing in a small bowl by combining the vinegar with the oil and mustard. Stir in the sesame seeds and herbs. Mix the dressing into the salad. Taste for seasoning, adding salt, pepper or more oil and vinegar as necessary. Stir in the cheese. Allow the salad to stand for 15 minutes before serving.

Pasta Salad with Olives

Insalata di pasta con olive

This delicious salad combines all the flavors of the Mediterranean. It is an excellent way of serving pasta and is particularly nice on hot summer days.

Ingredients

1 lb short pasta, such as medium shells,
    farfalle or penne
4 tbsp extra-virgin olive oil
10 sun-dried tomatoes, thinly sliced
2 tbsp capers, in brine or salted
⅔ cup black olives, pitted
2 cloves garlic, finely chopped
3 tbsp balsamic vinegar
salt and freshly ground black pepper
3 tbsp chopped fresh parsley
serves 6

3 ▲ Combine the olives, tomatoes, capers, garlic and vinegar in a small bowl. Season with salt and pepper.

4 ▲ Stir this mixture into the pasta, and toss well. Add 2 or 3 spoons of the tomato soaking water if the salad seems too dry. Toss with the parsley, and allow to stand for 15 minutes before serving.

1 ▲ Cook the pasta in a large pan of rapidly boiling salted water until it is *al dente*. Drain, and rinse under cold water to stop the cooking. Drain well and turn into a large bowl. Toss with the olive oil, and set aside.

2 ▲ Soak the tomatoes in a bowl of hot water for 10 minutes. Do not discard the water. Rinse the capers well. If they have been preserved in salt, soak them in a little hot water for 10 minutes. Rinse again.

Fettuccine with Ham and Cream
Fettuccine con prosciutto

Prosciutto is perfect for this rich and delicious dish, which makes an elegant first course.

Ingredients
1 × 4 oz slice prosciutto crudo or other
   unsmoked ham
¼ cup butter
2 shallots, very finely chopped
salt and freshly ground black pepper
¾ cup heavy cream
12 oz fettuccine
½ cup grated Parmesan cheese
sprig fresh parsley, to garnish
serves 4

2 ▲ Melt the butter in a medium frying pan, and add the shallots and the squares of ham fat. Cook until golden. Add the lean ham, and cook for 2 minutes more. Season with black pepper. Stir in the cream, and keep warm over low heat while the pasta is cooking.

3 ▲ Boil the pasta in a large pan of rapidly boiling salted water. Drain when *al dente*. Turn into a warmed serving bowl, and toss with the sauce. Stir in the cheese and serve at once, garnished with a sprig of parsley.

~ VARIATION ~

Substitute 6 oz fresh or frozen peas for the ham. Add to the pan with the shallots.

1 ▲ Cut the fat from the ham, and chop both lean and fat parts separately into small squares.

Tagliatelle with Smoked Salmon
Tagliatelle con salmone affumicato

In Italy smoked salmon is imported, and quite expensive. This elegant creamy sauce makes a little go a long way. Use a mixture of green and white pasta if you wish.

Ingredients
¾ cup smoked salmon slices or ends,
   fresh or frozen
1¼ cups light cream
pinch of ground mace or nutmeg
12 oz green and white tagliatelle
salt and freshly ground black pepper
3 tbsp chopped fresh chives, to garnish
serves 4–5

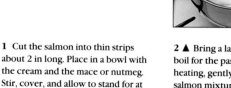

1 Cut the salmon into thin strips about 2 in long. Place in a bowl with the cream and the mace or nutmeg. Stir, cover, and allow to stand for at least 2 hours in a cool place.

2 ▲ Bring a large pan of water to a boil for the pasta. While the water is heating, gently warm the cream and salmon mixture in a small saucepan without boiling it.

3 ▲ Add salt to the boiling water. Drop in the pasta all at once. Drain when it is just *al dente*. Pour the sauce over the pasta and mix well. Season and garnish with the chives.

Baked Lasagne with Meat Sauce

Lasagne al forno

This lasagne made from egg pasta with home-made meat and béchamel sauces is exquisite.

Ingredients
1 recipe Bolognese Meat Sauce
egg pasta sheets made with 3 eggs, or
    1 lb dried lasagne
1 cup grated Parmesan cheese
3 tbsp butter
For the béchamel sauce
3 cups milk
1 bay leaf
3 blades mace
½ cup butter
¾ cup flour
salt and freshly ground black pepper
serves 8–10

1 Prepare the meat sauce and set aside. Butter a large shallow baking dish, preferably rectangular or square.

2 Make the béchamel sauce by gently heating the milk with the bay leaf and mace in a small saucepan. Melt the butter in a medium heavy saucepan. Add the flour, and mix it in well with a wire whisk. Cook for 2–3 minutes. Strain the hot milk into the flour and butter, and mix smoothly with the whisk. Bring the sauce to a boil, stirring constantly, and cook for 4–5 minutes more. Season with salt and pepper, and set aside.

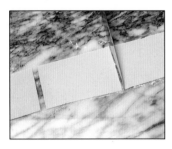

3 ▲ Make the pasta. Do not let it dry out before cutting it into rectangles approximately 4½ in wide and the same length as the baking dish (this will make it easier to assemble). Preheat the oven to 400°F.

4 ▲ Bring a very large pan of water to a boil. Place a large bowl of cold water near the stove. Cover a large work surface with a tablecloth. Add salt to the rapidly boiling water. Drop in 3 or 4 of the egg pasta rectangles. Cook very briefly, about 30 seconds. Remove them from the pan using a slotted spoon, and drop them into the bowl of cold water for about 30 seconds. Pull them out of the water, shaking off the excess water. Lay them out flat without overlapping on the tablecloth. Continue with all the remaining pasta and trimmings.

5 ▲ To assemble the lasagne, have all the elements at hand: the baking dish, béchamel and meat sauces, pasta strips, grated Parmesan and butter. Spread one large spoonful of the meat sauce over the bottom of the dish. Arrange a layer of pasta in the dish, cutting it with a sharp knife so that it fits well inside the dish.

6 ▲ Cover with a thin layer of meat sauce, then one of béchamel. Sprinkle with a little cheese. Repeat the layers in the same order, ending with a layer of pasta coated with béchamel. Do not make more than about 6 layers of pasta. (If you have a lot left over, make another small lasagne in a little ovenproof dish.) Use the pasta trimmings to patch any gaps in the pasta. Sprinkle the top with Parmesan, and dot with butter.

7 Bake in the preheated oven for 20 minutes or until brown on top. Remove from the oven and allow to stand for 5 minutes before serving. Serve directly from the baking dish, cutting out rectangular or square sections for each helping.

~ VARIATION ~

If you are using dried or bought pasta, follow step 4, but boil the lasagne in just two batches, and stop the cooking about 4 minutes before the recommended cooking time on the package has elapsed. Rinse in cold water and lay the pasta out the same way as for the egg pasta.

Tagliolini with Asparagus

Tagliolini con asparagi

Tagliolini are very thin home-made egg noodles, more delicate in texture than spaghetti. They go well with this subtle cream sauce flavored with asparagus.

Ingredients

1 lb fresh asparagus
egg pasta sheets made with 2 eggs, or
    12 oz fresh tagliolini or other egg
    noodles
¼ cup butter
3 scallions, finely chopped
3–4 leaves fresh mint or basil, finely
    chopped
⅔ cup heavy cream
salt and freshly ground black pepper
½ cup freshly grated Parmesan or
    Romano cheese
serves 4

3 Make the egg pasta sheets, and fold and cut into thin noodles, or feed them through the narrowest cutters of a machine. Open the noodles out, and let them dry for at least 5–10 minutes.

5 Bring the asparagus cooking water back to the boil. Add salt. Drop the noodles in all at once. Cook until just tender (freshly made noodles will cook in a few seconds). Drain.

4 ▲ Melt the butter in a large frying pan. Add the scallions and herbs, and cook for 3–4 minutes. Stir in the cream and asparagus, and heat gently, but do not boil. Season to taste.

6 ▲ Turn the pasta into the pan with the sauce, raise heat slightly, and mix well. Stir in the Parmesan or Romano. Mix well and serve at once.

1 ▲ Peel the asparagus by inserting a small sharp knife at the base of the stalks and pulling upwards towards the tips. Drop them into a large pan or rapidly boiling water, and boil until just tender, 4–6 minutes.

2 ▲ Remove from the water, reserving the cooking water. Cut the tips off, and then cut the stalks into 1½ in pieces. Set aside.

Ravioli with Ricotta and Spinach
Ravioli ripieni di magro

Home-made ravioli are fun to make, and can be stuffed with different meat, cheese or vegetable fillings. This filling is easy to make, and lighter than the normal meat variety.

Ingredients
14 oz fresh spinach or 6 oz frozen spinach
¾ cup ricotta cheese
1 egg
½ cup grated Parmesan cheese
pinch of grated nutmeg
salt and freshly ground black pepper
egg pasta sheets made with 3 eggs
For the sauce
⅓ cup butter
5–6 sprigs fresh sage
serves 4

1 Wash fresh spinach well in several changes of water. Place in a saucepan with only the water that is clinging to the leaves. Cover, and cook until tender, about 5 minutes. Drain. Cook frozen spinach according to the instructions on the package. When the spinach is cool, squeeze out as much moisture as possible. Chop finely.

2 Combine the chopped spinach with the ricotta, egg, Parmesan and nutmeg. Mix well. Season with salt and pepper. Cover the bowl and set aside.

3 Prepare the sheets of egg pasta. Roll out very thinly by hand or machine. Do not let the pasta dry out.

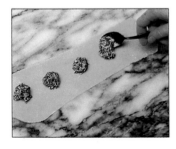

4 ▲ Place small teaspoons of filling along the pasta in rows 2 in apart. Cover with another sheet of pasta, pressing down gently to avoid forming air pockets.

5 ▲ Use a fluted pastry wheel to cut between the rows to form small squares with filling in the center of each. If the edges do not stick well, moisten with milk or water, and press together with a fork. Place the ravioli on a lightly floured surface, and allow to dry for at least 30 minutes. Turn occasionally so they dry on both sides. Bring a large pan of salted water to a boil.

6 Heat the butter and sage together over very low heat, taking care that the butter melts but does not darken.

7 ▲ Drop the ravioli into the boiling water. Stir gently to prevent them from sticking. They will be cooked in very little time, about 4–5 minutes. Drain carefully and arrange in individual serving dishes. Spoon on the sauce, and serve at once.

Baked Vegetable Lasagne

Lasagne al forno con funghi e pomodori

*Following the principles of the classic meat sauce lasagne, other combinations of ingredients
can be used most effectively. This vegetarian lasagne uses fresh vegetables and herbs.*

Ingredients

egg pasta sheets made with 3 eggs
2 tbsp olive oil
1 medium onion, very finely chopped
1¼ lb tomatoes, fresh or canned,
  chopped
salt and freshly ground black pepper
1½ lb cultivated or wild mushrooms, or a
  combination of both
⅓ cup butter
2 cloves garlic, finely chopped
juice of ½ lemon
4½ cups béchamel sauce
1½ cups freshly grated Parmesan or
  Romano cheese, or a combination
  of both
serves 8

1 Butter a large shallow baking dish,
preferably rectangular or square.

2 ▲ Make the egg pasta. Do not let it
dry out before cutting it into
rectangles approximately 4½ in wide
and the same length as the baking dish
(this will make it easier to assemble).

3 In a small frying pan heat the oil and
sauté the onion until translucent. Add
the chopped tomatoes, and cook for
6–8 minutes, stirring often. Season
with salt and pepper, and set aside.

4 ▲ Wipe the mushrooms carefully
with a damp cloth. Slice finely. Heat
2 tbsp of the butter in a frying pan, and
when it is bubbling, add the
mushrooms. Cook until the
mushrooms start to exude their juices.
Add the garlic and lemon juice, and
season with salt and pepper. Cook
until the liquids have almost all
evaporated and the mushrooms are
starting to brown. Set aside.

5 ▲ Preheat the oven to 400°F. Bring
a very large pan of water to a boil.
Place a large bowl of cold water near
the stove. Cover a large work surface
with a tablecloth. Add salt to the
rapidly boiling water. Drop in 3 or 4 of
the egg pasta rectangles. Cook very
briefly, about 30 seconds. Remove
them from the pan using a slotted
spoon, and drop them into the bowl of
cold water for about 30 seconds.
Remove and lay out to dry. Continue
with the remaining pasta.

6 ▲ To assemble the lasagne have all
the elements at hand: the baking dish,
fillings, pasta, cheeses and butter.
Spread one large spoonful of the
béchamel sauce over the bottom of
the dish. Arrange a layer of pasta in the
dish, cutting it with a sharp knife so
that it fits well. Cover the pasta with a
thin layer of mushrooms, then one of
béchamel sauce. Sprinkle with a little
Parmesan or Romano cheese.

7 ▲ Make another layer of pasta,
spread with a thin layer of tomatoes,
and then one of béchamel. Sprinkle
with cheese. Repeat the layers in the
same order, ending with a layer of
pasta coated with béchamel. Do not
make more than about 6 layers of
pasta. Use the pasta trimmings to patch
any gaps in the pasta. Sprinkle with
cheese, and dot with butter.

8 Bake for 20 minutes. Remove from
the oven and allow to stand for **5**
minutes before serving.

Tortelli with Pumpkin Stuffing
Tortelli di zucca

During autumn and winter the northern Italian markets are full of bright orange pumpkins, which are used to make soups and pasta dishes. This dish is a speciality of Mantua.

Ingredients
2 lb pumpkin (weight with shell)
1½ cups amaretti cookies, crushed fine
2 eggs
¾ cup freshly grated Parmesan or
    Romano cheese
pinch of grated nutmeg
salt and freshly ground black pepper
plain breadcrumbs, as required
egg pasta sheets made with 3 eggs
To serve
½ cup butter
¾ cup freshly grated Parmesan or
    Romano cheese
serves 6–8

1 Preheat the oven to 375°F. Cut the pumpkin into 4 in pieces. Leave the skin on. Place the pumpkin pieces in a covered casserole, and bake for 45–50 minutes. When cool, cut off the skins. Purée the flesh in a food mill or food processor or press through a sieve.

2 ▲ Combine the pumpkin purée with the cookie crumbs, eggs, cheese and nutmeg. Season with salt and pepper. If the mixture is too wet, add 1–2 tbsp of breadcrumbs. Set aside.

3 Prepare the sheets of egg pasta. Roll out very thinly by hand or machine. Do not let the pasta dry out before filling it.

4 ▲ Place tablespoons of filling every 2½ in along the pasta in rows 2 in apart. Cover with another sheet of pasta, and press down gently. Use a fluted pastry wheel to cut between the rows to form rectangles with filling in the center of each. Place the tortelli on a lightly floured surface, and allow to dry for at least 30 minutes. Turn them occasionally so they dry on both sides.

5 Bring a large pan of salted water to a boil. Gently heat the butter over very low heat, taking care that it does not darken.

6 ▲ Drop the tortelli into the boiling water. Stir to prevent from sticking. They will be cooked in 4–5 minutes. Drain and arrange in individual dishes. Spoon on the melted butter, sprinkle with Parmesan or Romano, and serve.

Stuffed Pasta Half-moons

Mezzelune ripiene di formaggi

These stuffed egg pasta half-moons are filled with a delicate mixture of cheeses. They make an elegant first course.

Ingredients

1¼ cups fresh ricotta or cottage cheese
1¼ cups mozzarella cheese
1 cup freshly grated Parmesan or
    Romano cheese
2 eggs
3 tbsp finely chopped fresh basil
salt and freshly ground black pepper
egg pasta sheets made with 3 eggs

For the sauce

1 lb fresh tomatoes
2 tbsp olive oil
1 small onion, very finely chopped
6 tbsp cream
serves 6–8

3 Prepare the sheets of egg pasta. Roll out very thinly by hand or machine. Do not let the pasta dry out.

4 ▲ Using a water glass or pastry cutter, cut out rounds approximately 4 in in diameter. Spoon one large tablespoon of the filling onto one half of each pasta round and fold over.

5 Press the edges closed with a fork. Re-roll any trimmings and use to make more rounds. Allow the half-moons to dry for at least 10–15 minutes. Turn them over so they dry evenly.

6 Bring a large pan of salted water to a boil. Place the tomato sauce in a small saucepan and heat gently while the pasta is cooking. Stir in the cream. Do not boil.

7 Gently drop in the stuffed pasta, and stir carefully to prevent them from sticking. Cook for 5–7 minutes. Scoop them out of the water, drain carefully, and arrange in individual dishes. Spoon on some of the sauce, and serve at once.

1 ▲ Press the ricotta or cottage cheese through a sieve or strainer. Chop the mozzarella into very small cubes. Combine all three cheeses in a bowl. Beat in the eggs and basil, season and set aside.

2 Make the sauce by dropping the tomatoes into a small pan of boiling water for 1 minute. Remove, and peel using a small sharp knife to pull the skins off. Chop the tomatoes finely. Heat the oil in a medium saucepan. Add the onion and cook over moderate heat until soft and translucent. Add the tomatoes and cook until soft, about 15 minutes. Season with salt and pepper. (The sauce may be pressed through a sieve to make it smooth.) Set aside.

Cannelloni Stuffed with Meat

Cannelloni ripieni di carne

Cannelloni are rectangles of home-made egg pasta which are spread with a filling, rolled up and baked in a sauce. In this recipe, they are baked in a béchamel sauce.

Ingredients

2 tbsp olive oil
1 medium onion, very finely chopped
1½ cups very lean ground beef
  (preferably 80% lean)
½ cup cooked ham (either boiled or
  baked), finely chopped
1 tbsp chopped fresh parsley
2 tbsp tomato paste, softened in 1 tbsp
  warm water
1 egg
salt and freshly ground black pepper
egg pasta sheets made with 2 eggs
3½ cups béchamel sauce
½ cup freshly grated Parmesan or
  Romano cheese
3 tbsp butter
serves 6–8

2 ▲ Remove from the heat, and turn the beef mixture into a bowl with the ham and parsley. Add the tomato paste and the egg, and mix well. Season with salt and pepper. Set aside.

1 ▲ Prepare the meat filling by heating the oil in a medium saucepan. Add the onion, and sauté gently until translucent. Stir in the beef, crumbling it with a fork, and stirring constantly until it has lost its raw red color. Cook for 3–4 minutes.

3 ▲ Make the egg pasta sheets with a machine or by hand. Do not let the pasta dry before cutting it into rectangles 5–6 in long and as wide as they come from the machine (3 in if you are not using a machine).

4 Bring a very large pan of water to a boil. Place a large bowl of cold water near the stove. Cover a large work surface with a tablecloth. Add salt to the rapidly boiling water. Drop in 3 or 4 of the egg pasta rectangles. Cook very briefly, about 30 seconds. Remove and drop them into the bowl of cold water for about 30 seconds more. Pull them out of the water, shaking off the excess water. Lay them out flat on the tablecloth. Continue with the remaining pasta.

5 Preheat the oven to 425°F. Select a shallow baking dish large enough to accommodate all the cannelloni in one layer. Butter the dish, and smear 2–3 tbsp of béchamel sauce over the bottom.

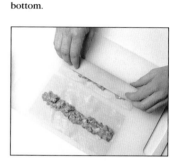

6.▲ Stir about one-third of the béchamel into the meat filling. Spread a thin layer of filling on each pasta rectangle. Roll the rectangles up loosely starting from the long side, jelly-roll style. Place the cannelloni into the baking dish with their open edges down.

7 ▲ Spoon the rest of the béchamel over the cannelloni, pushing a little down between each pasta roll. Sprinkle the top with the grated Parmesan or Romano, and dot with butter. Bake for about 20 minutes. Allow to rest for 5–8 minutes before serving.

RICE, POLENTA, EGGS AND CHEESE

Classic risottos are wonderfully creamy, flavored subtly with mushrooms, asparagus or shrimp. Thick yellow polenta goes well with meat or vegetable stews or cheeses and can be easily mastered by following the steps.

Risotto with Cheese

Risotto alla parmigiana

Risotto is distinguished from other rice dishes by its unique cooking method.

Ingredients
5½ cups beef, chicken or vegetable
    stock, preferably home-made
5 tbsp butter
1 small onion, finely chopped
1½ cups medium-grain risotto rice, such
    as arborio
½ cup dry white wine
salt and freshly ground black pepper
¾ cup freshly grated Parmesan or
    Romano cheese
serves 3–4

1 Heat the stock in a medium saucepan, and keep it simmering until it is needed.

2 In a large heavy frying pan or casserole, melt two-thirds of the butter. Stir in the onion, and cook gently until it is soft and golden. Add the rice, mixing it well to coat it with butter. After 1–2 minutes pour in the wine.

3 ▲ Raise the heat slightly, and cook until the wine evaporates. Add one small ladleful of the hot stock. Over moderate heat cook until the stock is absorbed or evaporates, stirring the rice with a wooden spoon to prevent it from sticking to the pan. Add a little more stock, and stir until the rice dries out again. Continue stirring and adding the liquid a little at a time. After about 20 minutes of cooking time, taste the rice. Add salt and pepper.

4 Continue cooking, stirring and adding the liquid until the rice is *al dente*, or tender but still firm to the bite. The total cooking time of the risotto may be from 20–35 minutes. If you run out of stock, use hot water, but do not worry if the rice is done before you have used up all the stock.

5 ▲ Remove the risotto pan from the heat. Stir in the remaining butter and the cheese. Taste again for seasoning. Allow the risotto to rest for 3–4 minutes before serving.

Risotto with Shrimp

Risotto con gamberi

This shrimp risotto is given a soft pink color by the addition of a little tomato paste.

Ingredients
12 oz fresh shrimp in their shells
5 cups water
1 bay leaf
1–2 sprigs of parsley
1 tsp whole peppercorns
2 cloves garlic, peeled
5 tbsp butter
2 shallots, finely chopped
1½ cups medium-grain risotto rice, such
    as arborio
1 tbsp tomato paste softened in ½ cup
    dry white wine
salt and freshly ground black pepper
serves 4

1 Place the shrimp in a large saucepan with the water, herbs, peppercorns and garlic. Bring to a boil and cook for about 1 minute. Remove the shrimp, peel, and return the shells to the saucepan. Boil the shells for another 10 minutes. Strain. Return the broth to a saucepan, and simmer until needed.

2 Slice the shrimp in half lengthwise, removing the dark vein along the back. Set 4 halves aside for garnish, and roughly chop the rest.

3 Heat two-thirds of the butter in a casserole. Add the shallots and cook until golden. Stir in the shrimp. Cook for 1–2 minutes.

4 ▲ Add the rice, mixing well to coat it with butter. After 1–2 minutes pour in the tomato paste and wine. Follow steps 3–5 for Risotto with Cheese, omitting the cheese and garnishing with the reserved prawn halves.

Risotto with Mushrooms

Risotto con funghi

The addition of wild mushrooms gives this risotto a wonderful woodsy flavor.

Ingredients

⅓ cup dried wild mushrooms, preferably
   porcini
1½ cups fresh cultivated mushrooms
juice of ½ lemon
⅓ cup butter
2 tbsp finely chopped parsley
4 cups beef or chicken stock, preferably
   home-made
2 tbsp olive oil
1 small onion, finely chopped
1½ cups medium-grain risotto rice, such
   as arborio
½ cup dry white wine
salt and freshly ground black pepper
3 tbsp freshly grated Parmesan or
   Romano cheese
serves 3–4

1 Place the dried mushrooms in a small bowl with about 1½ cups warm water. Soak for at least 40 minutes. Rinse the mushrooms thoroughly. Filter the soaking water through a strainer lined with paper towels, and reserve.

2 ▲ Wipe the fresh mushrooms with a damp cloth, and slice finely. Place in a bowl and toss with the lemon juice. In a large heavy frying pan or casserole melt one third of the butter. Stir in the fresh sliced mushrooms and cook over moderate heat until they give up their juices, and begin to brown. Stir in the parsley, cook for 30 seconds more, and remove to a side dish.

3 Place the stock in a saucepan. Add the mushroom water, and simmer until needed.

4 ▲ Heat another third of the butter with the olive oil in the same pan the mushrooms were cooked in. Stir in the onion, and cook until it is soft and golden. Add the rice, stirring for 1–2 minutes to coat it with the oils. Add the soaked and sautéed mushrooms, and mix well.

5 ▲ Pour in the wine, and cook over moderate heat until it evaporates. Follow steps 3–4 for Risotto with Cheese.

6 Remove the risotto pan from the heat. Stir in the remaining butter and the Parmesan or Romano. Grind in a little black pepper, and taste again for salt. Allow the risotto to rest for 3–4 minutes before serving.

Risotto with Asparagus

Risotto con asparagi

This is an elegant risotto to make when asparagus is in season.

Ingredients

8 oz fresh asparagus, peeled
3 cups vegetable or beef stock, preferably
    home-made
5 tbsp butter
1 small onion, finely chopped
2 cups medium-grain risotto rice, such
    as arborio
salt and freshly ground black pepper
¾ cup freshly grated Parmesan or
    Romano cheese

serves 4–5

1 Bring a large pan of water to a boil. Add the asparagus. Bring the water back to a boil, and blanch for 5 minutes. Lift the asparagus out, reserving the cooking water. Rinse the asparagus under cold water. Drain. Cut the asparagus diagonally into 1½ in pieces. Keep the tip and next-highest sections separate from the stalk sections.

2 Place the vegetable or beef stock in a saucepan. Measure out 3¾ cups of the asparagus cooking water, and add it to the stock. Heat the liquid to simmering, and keep it hot until it is needed.

4 ▲ Stir in half a ladleful of the hot liquid. Using a wooden spoon, stir constantly until the liquid has been absorbed or evaporated. Add another half ladleful of the liquid, and stir until it has been absorbed. Continue stirring and adding the liquid, a little at a time, for about 10 minutes.

5 ▲ Add the remaining asparagus sections, and proceed as for step 4 of Risotto with Cheese.

6 Remove the risotto pan from the heat. Stir in the remaining butter and the Parmesan or Romano. Grind in a little black pepper, and taste again for salt. Serve at once.

3 ▲ Heat two-thirds of the butter in a large heavy frying pan or casserole. Add the onion and cook until it is soft and golden. Stir in all the asparagus except the top two sections. Cook for 2–3 minutes. Add the rice, mixing well to coat it with butter for 1–2 minutes.

Polenta

Polenta

Polenta is a form of cornmeal. It is eaten in northern Italy in place of rice or pasta.

Ingredients
6¼ cups water
1 tbsp salt
2½ cups polenta
serves 4–6

1 ▲ Bring the water to a boil in a large heavy saucepan. Add the salt. Reduce the heat to a simmer, and begin to add the polenta in a fine rain. Stir constantly with a whisk until the polenta has all been incorporated.

2 ▲ Switch to a long-handled wooden spoon, and continue to stir the polenta over low to moderate heat until it is a thick mass, and pulls away from the sides of the pan. This may take from 25–50 minutes, depending on the type of polenta used. For best results, never stop stirring the polenta until you remove it from the heat.

3 ▲ When the polenta is cooked, spoon it into a large slightly wet bowl, wait 5 minutes, and turn it out onto a serving platter. Serve it with a meat or tomato sauce, or follow the instructions given in the recipes on the following pages.

Fried Polenta

Polenta fritta

Leftover polenta can be fried, making a crispy appetizer to serve with drinks or antipasti.

Ingredients
cold leftover polenta
oil, for deep-frying
flour, for dredging
salt and freshly ground black pepper
serves 6–8 as an appetizer

2 Heat the oil until a small piece of bread sizzles as soon as it is dropped in (about 360°F).

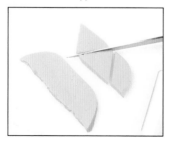

1 ▲ Cut the polenta into slices about ½ inch thick. Cut the slices into triangles or rounds.

3 ▲ Season the flour with salt and pepper. Dredge the pieces lightly in the flour, shaking off any excess.

4 ▲ Fry the polenta, a few pieces at a time, until golden and crisp. Drain on paper towels while the remaining pieces are frying. Serve at once.

Polenta with Mushrooms

Polenta con funghi

This dish is delicious made with a mixture of wild and cultivated mushrooms. Just a few dried porcini mushrooms will help to give cultivated mushrooms a more interesting flavor.

Ingredients
2 tbsp dried porcini mushrooms (omit if
    using wild mushrooms)
4 tbsp olive oil
1 small onion, finely chopped
1½ lb mushrooms, wild or cultivated, or a
    combination of both
2 cloves garlic, finely chopped
3 tbsp chopped fresh parsley
3 medium tomatoes, peeled and diced
1 tbsp tomato paste
¾ cup warm water
¼ tsp fresh thyme leaves, or ⅛ tsp
    dried thyme
1 bay leaf
salt and freshly ground black pepper
a few sprigs fresh parsley, to garnish
For the polenta
6¼ cups water
1 tbsp salt
2½ cups polenta
serves 6

3 ▲ Clean the fresh mushrooms by wiping them with a damp cloth. Cut into slices. When the onion is soft add the mushrooms to the pan. Stir over moderate to high heat until they give up their liquid. Add the garlic, parsley and diced tomatoes. Cook for 4–5 minutes more.

5 ▲ Bring the water to a boil in a large heavy saucepan. Add the salt. Reduce the heat to a simmer, and begin to add the polenta in a fine rain. Stir constantly with a whisk until the polenta has all been incorporated.

6 Switch to a long-handled wooden spoon, and continue to stir the polenta over low to moderate heat until it is a thick mass, and pulls away from the sides of the pan. This may take from 25–50 minutes, depending on the type of polenta used. For best results, never stop stirring the polenta until you remove it from the heat.

1 ▲ Soak the dried mushrooms, if using, in a bowl of warm water for 20 minutes. Remove the mushrooms with a slotted spoon, and rinse them well in several changes of cool water. Filter the soaking water through a layer of paper towels placed in a sieve, and reserve.

2 In a large frying pan heat the oil, and sauté the onion over low heat until soft and golden.

4 ▲ Soften the tomato paste in the warm water (use only ½ cup water if you are using dried mushrooms). Add it to the pan with the herbs. Add the dried mushrooms and soaking liquid, if using them. Mix well and season with salt and pepper. Lower the heat to low to moderate and cook for 15–20 minutes. Set aside while you make the polenta.

7 ▲ When the polenta has almost finished cooking, gently reheat the mushroom sauce. To serve, spoon the polenta onto a warmed serving platter. Make a well in the center. Spoon some of the mushroom sauce into the well, and garnish with parsley. Serve at once, passing the remaining sauce in a separate bowl.

Broiled Polenta with Gorgonzola

Polenta alla griglia

Broiled polenta is delicious, and is a good way of using up cold polenta. Try it with any soft flavorful cheese. Plain broiled polenta is a good accompaniment to stews and soups.

Ingredients
6¼ cups water
1 tbsp salt
2½ cups polenta
1¼ cups Gorgonzola or other cheese, at room temperature
serves 6–8 as a snack or appetizer

1 ▲ Bring the water to a boil in a large heavy-bottomed saucepan. Add the salt. Reduce the heat to a simmer, and begin to add the polenta in a fine rain. Stir constantly with a whisk until the polenta has all been incorporated.

2 ▲ Switch to a long-handled wooden spoon, and continue to stir the polenta over low to moderate heat until it is a thick mass, and pulls away from the sides of the pan. This may take from 25–50 minutes, depending on the type of cornmeal used. For best results, never stop stirring the polenta until you remove it from the heat.

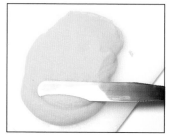

3 ▲ When the polenta is cooked, sprinkle a work surface or large board with a little water. Spread the polenta out onto the surface in a layer ¾ in thick. Allow to cool completely. Preheat the broiler.

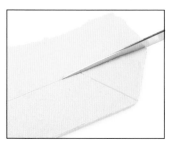

4 ▲ Cut the polenta into triangles. Broil until hot and speckled with brown on both sides. Spread with the Gorgonzola or other cheese. Serve immediately.

Polenta Baked with Cheese

Polenta pasticciata

Cold polenta can be cut into slices and baked in layers with cheese and other ingredients. The traditional way of cutting it is with a wooden knife or a piece of thick thread.

Ingredients

generous ⅓ cup butter
cooked polenta, made with 2 cups
    cornmeal
3 tbsp olive oil
2 medium onions, thinly sliced
pinch of grated nutmeg
salt and freshly ground black pepper
¾ cup mozzarella or sharp Cheddar
    cheese, cut into thin slices
3 tbsp finely chopped fresh parsley
⅓ cup freshly grated Parmesan or
    Romano cheese
serves 4–6

3 ▲ Season the onions with nutmeg, salt and pepper. Preheat the oven to 375°F. Butter an ovenproof dish. Spread a few of the onion slices in the bottom of the dish. Cover with a layer of the polenta rounds. Dot with butter.

4 ▲ Add a layer of the sliced mozzarella or Cheddar, and a sprinkling of parsley and Parmesan or Romano. Season with salt and pepper. Make another layer of the onions, and continue the layers in order, ending with the cheese. Dot the top with butter. Bake for 20–25 minutes, or until the cheese has melted. Serve from the baking dish.

1 ▲ Stir a third of the butter into the cooked polenta. Sprinkle a work surface with a little water. Spread the polenta out onto the surface in a layer ½ inch thick. Allow to cool. Cut the polenta into 2½ in rounds.

2 ▲ Heat the oil in a medium saucepan with 1 tbsp of the remaining butter. Add the onions, and stir over low heat until soft.

Timballo of Rice with Peas

Timballo di riso con piselli

The timballo is named because it looks like an inverted kettledrum (timballo or timpano).
It is made like a risotto, but is given a final baking in the oven, and then unmolded.

Ingredients
⅓ cup butter
2 tbsp olive oil
1 small onion, finely chopped
⅓ cup ham, cut into small dice
3 tbsp finely chopped fresh parsley, plus a few sprigs to garnish
2 cloves garlic, very finely chopped
1 cup shelled peas, fresh or frozen and thawed
salt and freshly ground black pepper
4 tbsp water
5½ cups fresh or canned beef or vegetable stock, preferably home-made (if canned, use a low-salt variety)
1½ cups medium-grain risotto rice, such as arborio
¾ cup freshly grated Parmesan or Romano cheese
¾ cup fontina cheese, very thinly sliced
a few sprigs parsley, to garnish
serves 4

1 ▲ Heat half the butter and all the oil in a large heavy frying pan or casserole. Add the onion, and cook for a few minutes until it softens. Add the ham, and stir over moderate heat for 3–4 minutes. Stir in the parsley and garlic. Cook for 1 or 2 minutes. Add the peas, mix well, season with salt and pepper and add the water. Cover the pan, and cook for about 8 minutes for fresh peas, 4 minutes for frozen peas. Remove the cover, and cook until all the liquid has evaporated. Remove half the pea mixture to a dish.

2 Heat the stock, and keep it simmering until needed. Butter a flat-bottomed ovenproof dish and line the bottom with a round of buttered waxed paper.

3 ▲ Stir the rice into the pea mixture. After 1–2 minutes, add a small ladleful of the hot broth. Cook over moderate heat until the broth is absorbed, stirring the rice with a wooden spoon to prevent it from sticking. Add a little more stock, and stir until the rice dries out again. Continue stirring and adding the liquid.

4 ▲ Preheat the oven to 350°F. After about 20 minutes of cooking time, taste the rice. As soon as the rice is just *al dente*, or tender but still firm to the bite, remove the pan from the heat. Correct the seasoning. Mix most of the remaining butter and half the grated Parmesan or Romano into the rice.

5 Assemble by sprinkling a little cheese into the bottom of the dish. Spoon about half the rice into the dish. Follow with a thin layer of the fontina and a layer of reserved cooked peas and ham. Sprinkle with cheese.

6 ▲ Cover with the remaining fontina slices and end with the rice. Sprinkle with cheese, and dot with butter. Bake in the preheated oven for 10–15 minutes. Remove from the oven, and allow to stand for 10 minutes.

7 ▲ To unmold, slip a knife around between the rice and the dish. Place a serving plate upside down on top of the dish. Wearing oven mitts, pick up the dish and turn it over while still holding the plate. If the rice does not drop down, give it a sharp knock with your gloved hand. Peel off the waxed paper. Garnish with parsley. Serve by cutting the timballo into wedges.

Fried Rice Balls Stuffed with Cheese *Supplì*

These deep-fried balls of risotto are stuffed with an inner filling of mozzarella cheese. They are very popular snacks in Rome and central Italy.

Ingredients

1 recipe Risotto with Parmesan Cheese
    or Risotto with Mushrooms
3 eggs
⅔ cup mozzarella cheese, cut into small
    dice
oil, for deep-frying
plain breadcrumbs, as required
flour, to coat
serves 4

3 Heat the oil until a small piece of bread sizzles as soon as it is dropped in (about 360°F).

4 ▲ Spread some flour on a plate. Beat the remaining egg in a shallow bowl. Sprinkle another plate with breadcrumbs. Roll the balls in the flour, then in the egg, and finally in the breadcrumbs.

5 ▲ Fry them a few at a time in the hot oil until golden and crisp. Drain on paper towels while the remaining balls are frying. Serve hot.

1 ▲ Allow the risotto to cool completely. (These are even better when formed from risotto made the day before.) Beat 2 of the eggs, and mix them well into the cold risotto.

2 ▲ Use your hands to form the rice mixture into balls the size of a large egg. If the mixture is too moist to hold its shape well, stir in a few tablespoons of breadcrumbs as necessary. Poke a hole into the center of each ball, fill it with a few small cubes of mozzarella, and close the hole over again with the rice mixture.

Potato Gnocchi

Gnocchi di patate

Gnocchi are little dumplings made either with mashed potato and flour, as here, or with semolina. They should be light in texture, and must not be overworked while being made.

Ingredients
2 lb waxy potatoes, scrubbed
1 tbsp salt
2–2½ cups flour
1 egg
pinch of grated nutmeg
2 tbsp butter
freshly grated Parmesan cheese, to serve
serves 4–6

1 Place the unpeeled potatoes in a large pot of salted water. Bring to a boil, and cook until the potatoes are tender but not falling apart. Drain. Peel as soon as possible, while the potatoes are still hot.

2 On a work surface spread out a layer of flour. Mash the hot potatoes with a food mill, dropping them directly onto the flour. Sprinkle with about half of the remaining flour and mix very lightly into the potatoes. Break the egg into the mixture, add the nutmeg, and knead lightly, drawing in more flour as necessary. When the dough is light to the touch and no longer moist or sticky it is ready to be rolled. Do not overwork or the gnocchi will be heavy.

3 ▲ Divide the dough into 4 parts. On a lightly floured board form each into a roll about ¾ inch in diameter. Cut the rolls crosswise into pieces about ¾ inch long.

4 ▲ Hold an ordinary table fork with long tines sideways, leaning on the board. One by one press and roll the gnocchi lightly along the tines of the fork towards the points, making ridges on one side, and a depression from your thumb on the other.

5 Bring a large pan of water to a fast boil. Add salt, and drop in about half the gnocchi.

6 ▲ When the gnocchi rise to the surface, after 3–4 minutes, the gnocchi are done. Scoop them out, allow to drain, and place in a warmed serving bowl. Dot with butter. Keep warm while the remaining gnocchi are boiling. As soon as they are cooked, toss the gnocchi with the butter or a heated sauce, sprinkle with grated Parmesan, and serve.

Potato and Spinach Gnocchi

Gnocchi di patate e spinaci

These green gnocchi are made in the same way as potato gnocchi, with the addition of fresh or frozen spinach. Serve tossed with butter or with a tomato sauce.

Ingredients

1½ lb fresh spinach, or 14 oz frozen leaf
    spinach
2 lb waxy potatoes, scrubbed
salt, to taste
2–2½ cups flour
1 egg
pinch of grated nutmeg
¼ cup butter
freshly grated Parmesan cheese, to serve
serves 6

1 Wash fresh spinach in several changes of cold water. Pull off any tough stalks. Place in a large saucepan with only the water that is clinging to the leaves. Cover the pan, and cook over moderate heat, stirring occasionally,until the spinach is tender, about 5–8 minutes. Cook uncovered for the last 2–3 minutes to boil off some of the water. Remove from the heat. Drain.

2 ▲ Cook frozen spinach according to the instructions on the package. Spread the spinach over a clean dish towel, roll it up and wring out all excess moisture. Chop the spinach finely with a sharp knife.

3 Place the unpeeled potatoes in a large pan of salted water. Bring to a boil, and cook until the potatoes are tender but not falling apart. Drain. Peel as soon as possible, while the potatoes are still hot.

4 ▲ On a work surface spread out a layer of flour. Mash the hot potatoes with a food mill, dropping them directly onto the flour. Add the spinach, and mix lightly into the potatoes. Sprinkle with about half of the remaining flour and mix in lightly.

5 Break the egg into the mixture, add the nutmeg, and knead lightly, drawing in more flour as necessary. When the dough is light to the touch and no longer moist or sticky it is ready to be rolled. Do not overwork or the gnocchi will be heavy.

6 ▲ Divide the dough into 4 parts. On a lightly floured board form each into a roll about ¾ inch in diameter. Cut the rolls crosswise into pieces about ¾ inch long.

7 ▲ Hold an ordinary table fork with long tines sideways, leaning on the board. One by one press and roll the gnocchi lightly along the tines of the fork towards the points, making ridges on one side, and a depression from your thumb on the other.

8 ▲ Bring a large pan of water to a fast boil. Add salt and drop about half the gnocchi in. They will sink to the bottom of the pan. When they rise to the surface, after 3–4 minutes, the gnocchi are done. Scoop them out with a large slotted spoon, and place in a warmed serving bowl. Keep warm while the remaining gnocchi are boiling. As soon as they are cooked, toss the gnocchi with the butter or a heated sauce, sprinkle with grated Parmesan, and serve.

Semolina Gnocchi

Gnocchi di semola

This famous Roman dish is made with coarsely ground semolina, which is cooked in a similar way to polenta. The rich paste is cut into flat discs, and baked with butter and cheese.

Ingredients
4½ cups milk
pinch of salt
3 tbsp butter
generous 2 cups coarsely ground
    semolina
3 egg yolks
3 tbsp freshly grated Parmesan or
    Romano cheese
For baking
5 tbsp butter, melted
½ cup freshly grated Parmesan or
    Romano cheese
pinch of grated nutmeg
serves 4

1 ▲ Heat the milk with the salt and a third of the butter in a heavy or non-stick saucepan. When it boils sprinkle in the semolina, stirring with a wire whisk to prevent lumps from forming. Bring the mixture to a boil. Lower heat and simmer for 15–20 minutes, stirring occasionally. The mixture will be very thick.

2 ▲ Remove from the heat and beat in the remaining butter, and then the egg yolks one at a time. Stir in the grated Parmesan or Romano. Season with salt. Sprinkle a little cold water onto a work surface. Spread the hot semolina mixture out onto it in an even layer about ½ inch thick. Allow to cool for at least 2 hours.

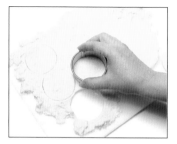

3 ▲ Preheat the oven to 425°F. Butter a shallow baking dish. Use a biscuit cutter to cut the semolina into 2½ in rounds.

4 ▲ Place the trimmings in an even layer in the bottom of the dish. Pour over a little melted butter, and sprinkle with cheese. Cover with a layer of the cut-out circles, overlapping them slightly. Sprinkle with nutmeg, cheese and butter. Continue the layering until all the ingredients have been used up.

5 Bake for about 20 minutes, or until the top is browned. Remove from the oven and allow to stand for 5 minutes before serving.

~ COOK'S TIP ~

Semolina is ground durum wheat, which is the kind used to make dried pasta. Buy semolina in small batches and store in an air-tight container as it goes stale when kept for too long.

Frittata with Sun-dried Tomatoes   *Frittata con pomodori secchi*

Adding just a few sun-dried tomatoes gives this frittata a distinctly Mediterranean flavor.

Ingredients
6 sun-dried tomatoes, dry or in oil and
    drained
4 tbsp olive oil
1 small onion, finely chopped
pinch of fresh thyme leaves
salt and freshly ground black pepper
6 eggs
½ cup freshly grated Parmesan or
    Romano cheese
serves 3–4

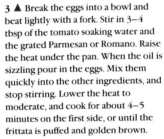

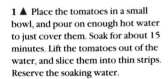

3 ▲ Break the eggs into a bowl and beat lightly with a fork. Stir in 3–4 tbsp of the tomato soaking water and the grated Parmesan or Romano. Raise the heat under the pan. When the oil is sizzling pour in the eggs. Mix them quickly into the other ingredients, and stop stirring. Lower the heat to moderate, and cook for about 4–5 minutes on the first side, or until the frittata is puffed and golden brown.

4 ▲ Take a large plate, place it upside down over the pan, and holding it firmly with oven mitts, turn the pan and the frittata over onto it. Slide the frittata back into the pan, and continue cooking until golden brown on the second side, 3–4 minutes more. Remove from the heat. The frittata can be served hot, at room temperature, or cold. Cut it into wedges to serve.

1 ▲ Place the tomatoes in a small bowl, and pour on enough hot water to just cover them. Soak for about 15 minutes. Lift the tomatoes out of the water, and slice them into thin strips. Reserve the soaking water.

2 ▲ Heat the oil in a large non-stick or heavy frying pan. Stir in the onion, and cook for 5–6 minutes or until soft and golden. Add the tomatoes and thyme, and stir over moderate heat for 2–3 minutes. Season with salt and pepper.

Frittata of Leftover Pasta

Frittata di pasta avanzata

This is a great way to use up cold leftover pasta, whatever the sauce.

Ingredients
5–6 eggs
1½–2 cups cold cooked pasta, with any
  sauce
½ cup freshly grated Parmesan cheese
salt and freshly ground black pepper
5 tbsp butter
serves 4

2 ▲ Heat half the butter in a large non-stick or heavy frying pan. As soon as the foam subsides pour in the pasta mixture. Cook over moderate heat, without stirring, for 4–5 minutes, or until the bottom is golden brown. Loosen the frittata by shaking the pan backwards and forwards.

3 ▲ Take a large plate, place it upside down over the pan and, holding it firmly with oven mitts, turn the pan and the frittata over onto it. Add the remaining butter to the pan. As soon as it stops foaming slide the frittata back into the pan, and continue cooking until golden brown on the second side, 3–4 minutes more. Remove from the heat. The frittata can be served hot, at room temperature, or cold. Cut it into wedges to serve.

1 ▲ In a medium bowl beat the eggs lightly with a fork. Stir in the pasta and the Parmesan. Season to taste.

Frittata with Onions

Frittata con cipolle

Gently cooked onions add a sweet flavor to the basic frittata mixture.

Ingredients
4 tbsp olive oil
2 medium onions, thinly sliced
salt and freshly ground black pepper
2 tbsp chopped fresh parsley or basil
6 eggs
serves 3–4

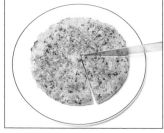

1 Heat the oil in a large non-stick or heavy frying pan. Stir in the onions, and cook over low heat until they are soft and golden. This may take 10–15 minutes. Season with salt and pepper. Stir in the herbs.

2 Break the eggs into a bowl, and beat them lightly with a fork. Raise the heat under the onions to moderate, and when they are sizzling pour in the eggs. Quickly stir them into the onions to distribute them. Stop stirring.

3 ▲ Cook for about 5 minutes on the first side, or until the frittata is puffed and golden brown. If the frittata seems to be sticking to the pan, shake the pan back and forth to release it.

4 ▲ Take a large plate, place it upside down over the pan and, holding it firmly with oven mitts, turn the pan and the frittata over onto it. Slide the frittata back into the pan, and continue cooking until golden brown on the second side, 3–4 minutes more. Remove from the heat. Cut it into wedges to serve.

Frittata with Spinach and Ham
Frittata con spinaci e prosciutto

In Italy, frittate are often used as fillings for sandwiches. This hearty version would make an excellent filling.

Ingredients

1 cup cooked leaf spinach, fresh or frozen
3 tbsp olive oil
4 scallions, finely sliced
1 clove garlic, finely chopped
⅓ cup ham or prosciutto, cut into small dice
salt and freshly ground black pepper
8 eggs

serves 6

3 ▲ Break the eggs into a bowl and beat lightly with a fork. Raise the heat under the vegetables. After about 1 minute pour in the eggs. Mix them quickly into the other ingredients, and stop stirring. Cook over moderate heat for about 5–6 minutes on the first side, or until the frittata is puffed and golden brown. If the frittata seems to be sticking to the pan, shake the pan backwards and forwards to release it.

4 ▲ Take a large plate, place it upside down over the pan and, holding it firmly with oven mitts, turn the pan and the frittata over onto it. Slide the frittata back into the pan, and continue cooking until golden brown on the second side, 3–4 minutes more. Remove from the heat. The frittata can be served hot, at room temperature, or cold. Cut it into wedges to serve.

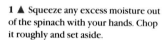

1 ▲ Squeeze any excess moisture out of the spinach with your hands. Chop it roughly and set aside.

2 ▲ Heat the oil in a large non-stick or heavy frying pan. Stir in the scallions, and cook for 3–4 minutes. Add the garlic and ham, and stir over moderate heat until just golden. Stir in the spinach, and cook for 3–4 minutes, or until just heated through. Season with salt and pepper.

Sliced Frittata Salad

Frittata fredda in insalata

This dish – cold frittata with a tomato sauce – is ideal for a light summer lunch.

Ingredients
6 eggs
2 tbsp mixed fresh herbs, very finely
    chopped, such as basil, parsley, thyme
    or tarragon
¼ cup freshly grated Parmesan or
    Romano cheese
salt and freshly ground black pepper
3 tbsp olive oil
For the tomato sauce
2 tbsp olive oil
1 small onion, finely chopped
12 oz fresh tomatoes, or 1 × 14 oz can
    tomatoes, chopped·
1 clove garlic, chopped
4 tbsp water
salt and freshly ground black pepper
serves 3–4

1 To make the frittata, break the eggs
into a bowl, and beat them lightly with
a fork. Beat in the herbs and cheese.
Season with salt and pepper. Heat the
oil in a large non-stick or heavy frying
pan until hot but not smoking.

2 ▲ Pour in the egg mixture. Cook,
without stirring, until the frittata is
puffed and golden brown underneath.

3 Take a large plate, place it upside
down over the pan, and holding it
firmly with oven mitts, turn the pan
and the frittata over onto it. Slide the
frittata back into the pan, and continue
cooking until golden brown on the
second side, 3–4 minutes more.
Remove from the heat and allow to
cool completely.

4 ▲ To make the tomato sauce, heat
the oil in a medium heavy saucepan.
Add the onion, and cook slowly until it
is soft. Add the tomatoes, garlic and
water, and season with salt and
pepper. Cover the pan and cook over
moderate heat until the tomatoes are
soft, about 15 minutes.

5 Remove from the heat, and cool
slightly before passing the sauce
through a food mill or strainer. Leave
to cool completely.

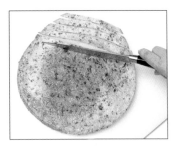

6 ▲ To assemble the salad, cut the
frittata into thin slices. Place them in a
serving bowl and toss lightly with the
sauce. Serve the salad at room
temperature or chilled.

Baked Eggs with Tomatoes

Uova al piatto con pomodori

These eggs simply baked over a fresh tomato sauce make an easy dish for a light supper.

Allow 1 or 2 eggs per person.

Ingredients
4 tbsp olive oil
1 small onion, finely chopped
1 lb tomatoes, peeled, seeded and
    chopped
2 tbsp chopped fresh basil
6 eggs
salt and freshly ground black pepper
1 tbsp butter
3 large or 6 small servings

1 ▲ Heat the oil in a shallow flameproof dish. Add the onion, and cook until soft and golden.

2 ▲ Preheat the oven to 375°F. Add the tomatoes to the onions, and cook for 5–10 minutes, or until the tomatoes are very soft. Stir in the chopped basil.

~ VARIATION ~

Sprinkle 2–3 tbsp of freshly grated Parmesan cheese over the eggs before baking for a richer, tastier dish.

3 ▲ Break the eggs, one at a time, and slip them into the dish in one layer on top of the tomatoes. Season with salt and pepper. Dot with butter. Cover the dish, and bake in the oven for 7–10 minutes, or until the egg whites have just set, but the yolks are still soft. Serve at once.

Baked Eggs with Cheese

Uova al piatto alla parmigiana

Grated Parmesan or Romano makes a tasty addition to this simple dish.

Ingredients
6 eggs
salt and freshly ground black pepper
3 tbsp baked or boiled ham, cut into thin
    matchsticks
6 tbsp freshly grated Parmesan or·
    Romano cheese
2 tbsp butter
3–4 leaves fresh basil, to garnish
rounds of crusty bread, warmed, to serve
3 large or 6 small servings

1 Preheat the oven to 400°F. Butter a shallow ovenproof dish (or dishes, if you prefer to bake the eggs individually).

2 ▲ Break the eggs into the dish. Season with salt and pepper. Sprinkle the ham over the whites. Sprinkle the top with the Parmesan or Romano.

3 ▲ Dot with butter. Cover the dish, and bake for 7–10 minutes, or until the whites have set and the cheese has melted. Garnish with the basil. Serve hot with warmed bread.

Fonduta with Steamed Vegetables *Fonduta con verdure*

*Fonduta is a creamy cheese sauce from the mountainous Val d'Aosta region. Traditionally it
is garnished with slices of white truffles and eaten with toasted bread rounds.*

Ingredients

assorted vegetables, such as fennel,
   broccoli, carrots, cauliflower and
   zucchini
½ cup butter
12–16 rounds of Italian or French
   baguette

For the fonduta

1⅔ cups fontina cheese
1 tbsp flour
milk, as required
¼ cup butter
½ cup freshly grated Parmesan or
   Romano cheese
pinch of grated nutmeg
salt and freshly ground black pepper
2 egg yolks, at room temperature
a few slivers of white truffle (optional)

serves 4

1 ▲ About 6 hours before you want to
serve the fonduta, cut the fontina into
chunks and place in a bowl. Sprinkle
with the flour. Pour in enough milk to
barely cover the cheese, and set aside
in a cool place. If you put the bowl in
the refrigerator, take it out at least 1
hour before cooking the fonduta. It
should be at room temperature before
being cooked.

2 Just before preparing the fonduta,
steam the vegetables until tender. Cut
into pieces. Place on a serving platter,
dot with butter, and keep warm.

3 Butter the rounds and toast them
lightly in the oven or the broiler.

4 ▲ For the fonduta, melt the butter
in a mixing bowl set over a pan of
simmering water, or in the top of a
double boiler. Strain the fontina and
add it, with 3–4 tbsp of its soaking
milk. Cook, stirring, until the cheese
melts. When it is hot, and has formed a
homogenous mass, add the Parmesan
or Romano and stir until melted.
Season with nutmeg, salt and pepper.

5 ▲ Remove from the heat and
immediately beat in the egg yolks
which have been passed through a
strainer. Spoon into warmed
individual serving bowls, garnish with
the white truffle if using, and serve
with the vegetables and toasted bread.

Fried Mozzarella

Mozzarella fritta

These cheese slices make a good informal lunch. They originate from the Neapolitan area, where much mozzarella is produced. They must be made just before serving.

Ingredients

1¾ cups mozzarella cheese
oil, for deep-frying
2 eggs
flour seasoned with salt and freshly
    ground black pepper, for coating
plain dry breadcrumbs, for coating
serves 2–3

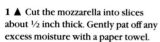

3 ▲ Press the cheese slices into the flour, coating them evenly with a thin layer of flour. Shake off any excess. Dip them into the egg, then into the breadcrumbs. Dip them once more into the egg, and then again into the breadcrumbs.

4 ▲ Fry immediately in the hot oil until golden brown. (You may have to do this in two batches but do not let the breaded cheese wait for too long or the breadcrumb coating will separate from the cheese while it is being fried.) Drain quickly on paper towels, and serve hot.

1 ▲ Cut the mozzarella into slices about ½ inch thick. Gently pat off any excess moisture with a paper towel.

2 ▲ Heat the oil until a small piece of bread sizzles as soon as it is dropped in (about 360°F). While the oil is heating beat the eggs in a shallow bowl. Spread some flour on one plate, and some breadcrumbs on another.

Grilled Cheese Sandwiches

Panini alla griglia

Garlic, herbs and tomatoes make these open sandwiches very Mediterranean.

Ingredients
3 tbsp olive oil
4 or 5 canned plum tomatoes, finely
    chopped
a few leaves fresh basil, torn into pieces
salt and freshly ground black pepper
4–6 medium slices of Italian or crusty
    bread
1 clove garlic, peeled and cut in half
½ cup scamorza, mozzarella or Cheddar
    cheese
serves 4

1 Heat the oil in a small frying pan. Add the tomatoes and basil, and season with salt and pepper. Cook over low to moderate heat for about 8–10 minutes, or until the tomatoes start to dry out. Preheat the broiler.

2 ▲ Lightly toast the bread. When it has cooled slightly rub it on one side with the garlic.

3 ▲ Spread some of the tomatoes on each piece of bread, and top with the sliced cheese. Place under the hot broiler until the cheese melts and begins to bubble, 5–8 minutes. Serve hot.

Mozzarella, Tomato and Basil Salad

Insalata caprese

This very popular and easy salad is considered rather patriotic in Italy, as its three ingredients are the colors of the national flag.

Ingredients
4 large tomatoes
2 cups mozzarella cheese, from cow or
    buffalo milk
8–10 leaves fresh basil
4 tbsp extra-virgin olive oil
salt and freshly ground black pepper
serves 4

2 ▲ Arrange the tomatoes and cheese in overlapping slices on a serving dish. Decorate with basil.

3 ▲ Sprinkle with olive oil and a little salt. Serve with the black pepper passed separately.

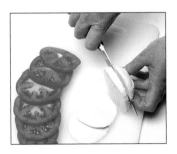

1 ▲ Slice the tomatoes and mozzarella into thick rounds.

~ COOK'S TIP ~

In Italy the most sought-after mozzarella is made from the milk of water buffalo. It is found mainly in the south and in Campania.

PIZZAS, PASTRIES AND BREAD

Pizzas are fun to make at home. Personalize them with combinations of your favorite ingredients. Italian flatbreads and breadsticks can be topped with herbs and seeds for tasty accompaniments or starters or unusual snacks.

Basic Pizza Dough

Pizza dough is leavened with yeast. It usually rises once before being rolled out and filled. The dough can be baked in pizza pans or baked directly on a flat cookie sheet.

Ingredients

2½ tbsp fresh cake yeast or 1 package dry yeast
1 cup lukewarm water
pinch of sugar
1 tsp salt
3–3½ cups unbleached white flour
serves 4 as a main course or 8 as an appetizer

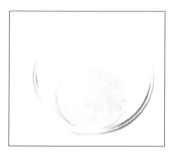

1 ▲ Warm a medium mixing bowl by swirling some hot water in it. Drain. Place the yeast in the bowl, and pour on the warm water. Stir in the sugar, mix with a fork, and allow to stand until the yeast has dissolved and starts to foam, 5–10 minutes.

2 ▲ Use a wooden spoon to mix in the salt and about one-third of the flour. Mix in another third of the flour, stirring with the spoon until the dough forms a mass and begins to pull away from the sides of the bowl.

3 ▲ Sprinkle some of the remaining flour onto a smooth work surface. Remove the dough from the bowl and begin to knead it, working in the remaining flour a little at a time. Knead for 8–10 minutes. By the end the dough should be elastic and smooth. Form it into a ball.

4 Lightly oil a mixing bowl. Place the dough in the bowl. Stretch a moistened and wrung-out dish towel across the top of the bowl, and leave it to stand in a warm place until the dough has doubled in volume, about 40–50 minutes or more, depending on the type of yeast used. (If you do not have a warm enough place, turn the oven on to medium heat for 10 minutes before you knead the dough. Turn it off. Place the bowl with the dough in it in the turned-off oven with the door closed and let it rise there.) To test whether the dough has risen enough, poke two fingers into the dough. If the indentations remain, the dough is ready.

5 ▲ Punch the dough down with your fist to release the air. Knead for 1–2 minutes.

6 If you want to make 2 medium pizzas, divide the dough into 2 balls. If you want to make 4 individual pizzas (in pans 10½ in in diameter), divide the dough into 4 balls. Pat the ball of dough out into a flat circle on a lightly floured surface. With a rolling pin, roll it out to a thickness of about ⅜–¼ inch. If you are using a pizza pan, roll the dough out about ¼ inch larger than the size of the pan for the rim of the crust.

7 ▲ Place in the lightly oiled pan, folding the extra dough under to make a thicker rim around the edge. If you are baking the pizza without a round pan, press some of the dough from the center of the circle towards the edge, to make a thicker rim. Place it on a lightly oiled flat cookie sheet. The dough is now ready for filling.

~ COOK'S TIP ~

This basic dough can be used for other recipes in this book, such as Focaccia, Breadsticks, Calzone and Sicilian Closed Pizza. The dough may be frozen at the end of step 7, and thawed before filling.

Wholewheat Pizza Dough

Pizza dough can also be made with wholewheat flour, although it is easier to handle and more elastic if a proportion of white flour is used. This dough can be used in any recipe calling for Basic Pizza Dough.

Ingredients
2½ tbsp fresh cake yeast or 1½ tbsp active dried yeast
1 cup lukewarm water
pinch of sugar
2 tbsp olive oil
1 tsp salt
1¼ cups plain white flour
2 cups stoneground wholewheat flour
serves 4 as a main course or 8 as an appetizer

1 Warm a medium mixing bowl by swirling some hot water in it. Drain. Place the yeast in the bowl, and pour on the warm water. Stir in the sugar, mix with a fork, and allow to stand until the yeast has dissolved and starts to foam, 5–10 minutes.

3 ▲ Proceed with steps 3–7 as for Basic Pizza Dough, punching down the risen dough, and kneading until ready to roll out and place in a pan.

2 ▲ Use a wooden spoon to mix in the olive oil and the salt, and the white flour. Mix in about half of the whole-wheat flour, stirring with the spoon until the dough forms a mass and begins to pull away from the sides of the bowl.

To Make the Dough in a Food Processor

1 ▲ Have all the ingredients ready and measured out. In a small jug or bowl add the yeast to the warm water. Stir in the sugar, and allow to stand until the yeast has dissolved, 5–10 minutes.

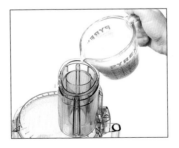

2 ▲ Fit the food processor with the metal blades. Place the salt and three-quarters of the flour in the bowl of the food processor. Turn it on, and pour in the yeast mixture and olive oil through the opening at the top. Continue processing until the dough forms one or two balls. Turn the machine off, open it, and touch the dough. If it still feels sticky, add a little more flour, and process again until it is incorporated.

3 ▲ Remove the dough from the processor. Knead it for about 2–3 minutes on a surface dusted with the remaining flour. Form it into a ball. Proceed with Step 4 of Basic Pizza Dough.

Cheese and Tomato Pizza
Pizza alla Margherita

The Margherita is named after the nineteenth-century Queen of Italy, and is one of the most popular of all pizzas.

Ingredients
1 lb peeled plum tomatoes, fresh or canned, weighed whole, without extra juice
1 recipe Basic Pizza Dough, rolled out
1¾ cups mozzarella cheese, cut into small dice
10–12 leaves fresh basil, torn into pieces
4 tbsp freshly grated Parmesan cheese (optional)
salt and freshly ground black pepper
3 tbsp olive oil
serves 4

1 Preheat the oven to 475°F for at least 20 minutes before baking. Strain the tomatoes through the medium holes of a food mill placed over a bowl, scraping in all the pulp.

2 ▲ Spread the puréed tomatoes onto the prepared pizza dough, leaving the rim uncovered.

3 ▲ Sprinkle evenly with the mozzarella. Dot with basil. Sprinkle with Parmesan if using, salt and pepper and olive oil. Immediately place the pizzas in the oven. Bake for about 15–20 minutes, or until the crust is golden brown and the cheeses melted and are bubbling.

Pizza with Mozzarella and Anchovies
Pizza alla napoletana

If you ask for a pizza in the Neapolitan manner anywhere in Italy other than in Naples, you will be given this pizza with anchovies.

Ingredients
1 lb peeled plum tomatoes, fresh or canned, weighed whole, without extra juice
1 recipe Basic Pizza Dough, rolled out
3 tbsp anchovy fillets in oil, drained and cut into pieces
1¾ cups mozzarella cheese, cut into small dice
1 tsp oregano leaves, fresh or dried
salt and freshly ground black pepper
3 tbsp olive oil
serves 4

1 Preheat the oven to 475°F for at least 20 minutes before baking. Strain the tomatoes through the medium holes of a food mill placed over a bowl, scraping in all the pulp.

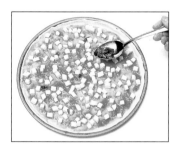

2 ▲ Spread the puréed tomatoes on the pizza dough, leaving the rim uncovered. Dot with the anchovy pieces and the mozzarella.

3 ▲ Sprinkle with oregano, salt and pepper, and olive oil. Immediately place the pizza in the oven. Bake for about 15–20 minutes, or until the crust is golden brown and the cheese is bubbling.

Four Seasons Pizza

Pizza quattro stagioni

The topping on this pizza is divided into four quarters, one for each "season". You may substitute suggested ingredients for any other seasonal flavors.

Ingredients

1 lb peeled plum tomatoes, fresh or
   canned, weighed whole, without
   extra juice
5 tbsp olive oil
1 cup cultivated mushrooms, thinly sliced
1 clove garlic, finely chopped
1 recipe Basic Pizza Dough, rolled out
1¾ cups mozzarella cheese, cut into
   small dice
4 thin slices of ham, cut into 2 in squares
32 black olives, pitted and halved
8 artichoke hearts marinated in oil,
   drained and cut in half
1 tsp oregano leaves, fresh or dried
salt and freshly ground black pepper
serves 4

1 ▲ Preheat the oven to 475°F for at least 20 minutes before baking the pizza. Strain the tomatoes through the medium holes of a food mill placed over a bowl, scraping in all the pulp.

2 Heat 2 tbsp of the oil and lightly sauté the mushrooms. Stir in the garlic and set aside.

3 ▲ Spread the puréed tomato on the prepared pizza dough, leaving the rim uncovered. Sprinkle evenly with the mozzarella. Spread mushrooms over one-quarter of each pizza.

4 ▲ Arrange the ham on another quarter, and the olives and artichoke hearts on the two remaining quarters. Sprinkle with oregano, salt and pepper, and the remaining olive oil. Immediately place the pizza in the oven. Bake for about 15–20 minutes, or until the crust is golden brown and the topping is bubbling.

Pizza with Fresh Vegetables

Pizza all'ortolana

This pizza can be made with any combination of fresh vegetables. Most will benefit from being blanched or sautéed before being baked on the pizza.

Ingredients
14 oz peeled plum tomatoes, fresh or
　　canned, weighed whole, without extra
　　juice
2 medium broccoli spears
8 oz fresh asparagus
2 small zucchini
5 tbsp olive oil
⅓ cup shelled peas, fresh or frozen
4 scallions, sliced
1 recipe Basic Pizza Dough, rolled out
½ cup mozzarella cheese, cut into small
　　dice
10 leaves fresh basil, torn into pieces
2 cloves garlic, finely chopped
salt and freshly ground black pepper
serves 4

4 ▲ Spread the puréed tomatoes onto the pizza dough, leaving the rim uncovered. Add the other vegetables, spreading them evenly over the tomatoes.

5 ▲ Sprinkle with the mozzarella, basil, garlic, salt and pepper, and remaining olive oil. Immediately place the pizza in the oven. Bake for about 20 minutes, or until the crust is golden brown and the cheese has melted.

1 Preheat the oven to 475°F for at least 20 minutes before baking the pizza. Strain the tomatoes through the medium holes of a food mill placed over a bowl, scraping in all the pulp.

2 ▲ Peel the broccoli stems and asparagus, and blanch with the zucchini in a large pan of boiling water for 4–5 minutes. Drain. Cut into bite-size pieces.

3 Heat 2 tbsp of the olive oil in a small pan. Stir in the peas and scallions, and cook for 5–6 minutes, stirring often. Remove from the heat.

Pizza with Sausage

Pizza con salsicce

Use sausages with a high meat content for this topping.

Ingredients
1 lb peeled plum tomatoes, fresh or
  canned, weighed whole, without extra
  juice
1 recipe Basic Pizza Dough, rolled out
1¾ cups mozzarella cheese, cut into
  small dice
1½ cups sausage meat, removed from
  the casings and crumbled
1 tsp oregano leaves, fresh or dried
salt and freshly ground black pepper
3 tbsp olive oil
serves 4

1 Preheat the oven to 475°F for at
least 20 minutes before baking the
pizza. Strain the tomatoes through the
medium holes of a food mill placed
over a bowl, scraping in all the pulp.

2 ▲ Spread some of the puréed
tomatoes on the prepared pizza
dough, leaving the rim uncovered.
Sprinkle evenly with the mozzarella.
Add the sausage meat in a layer.

3 ▲ Sprinkle with oregano, salt and
pepper, and olive oil. Immediately
place the pizza in the preheated oven.
Bake for about 15–20 minutes, or until
the crust is golden brown and the
cheese is bubbling.

Pizza with Four Cheeses

Pizza con quattro formaggi

Any combination of cheeses can be used, but choose cheeses which are different in character.

Ingredients
1 recipe Basic Pizza Dough, rolled out
½ cup Gorgonzola or other blue cheese,
  thinly sliced
½ cup mozzarella cheese, finely diced
½ cup goats cheese, thinly sliced
½ cup sharp Cheddar cheese, coarsely
  grated
4 leaves fresh sage, torn into pieces, or
  3 tbsp chopped fresh parsley
salt and freshly ground black pepper
3 tbsp olive oil
serves 4

1 Preheat the oven to 475°F for at
least 20 minutes before baking the
pizza. Arrange the Gorgonzola on one
quarter of the pizza and the mozzarella
on another, leaving the edge free.

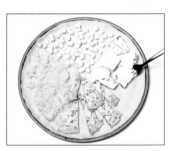

2 ▲ Arrange the goats and Cheddar
cheeses on the remaining two
quarters.

~ VARIATION ~

For an unusual taste, substitute
3 oz of sliced smoked cheese for
one of the other cheeses.

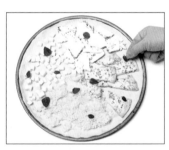

3 ▲ Sprinkle with the herbs, salt and
pepper, and olive oil. Immediately
place the pizza in the oven. Bake for
about 15–20 minutes, or until the
crust is golden brown and the cheeses
are bubbling.

Mediterranean Pizza

Pizza mediterranea

The combination of sweet and salty Mediterranean ingredients makes a delicious modern pizza topping.

Ingredients
12 sun-dried tomatoes, dry or in oil,
   drained
1¾ cups goats cheese, sliced as thinly as
   possible
1 recipe Basic Pizza Dough, rolled out
2 tbsp capers in brine or salt, rinsed
10 leaves fresh basil
salt and freshly ground black pepper
3 tbsp olive oil
serves 4

1 Preheat the oven to 475°F for at least 20 minutes before baking the pizza. Place the tomatoes in a small bowl, cover with hot water, and leave to soak for 15 minutes. Drain and cut into thin slices. (The soaking water may be saved to add to a pasta sauce or soup.)

2 ▲ Arrange the cheese on the prepared pizza dough in one layer, leaving the rim uncovered. Dot with the tomato slices.

3 ▲ Sprinkle with the capers and basil leaves. Allow to rise for 10 minutes before baking.

4 Sprinkle with salt, pepper and olive oil. Place the pizza in the oven. Bake for about 15–20 minutes, or until the crust is golden brown.

Pizza with Onions and Olives

Pizza con cipolle e olive

Onions cooked slowly to release their sweetness contrast with the salty bitterness of the olives.

Ingredients
6 tbsp olive oil
4 medium onions, finely sliced
salt and freshly ground black pepper
1 recipe Basic Pizza Dough, rolled out
1¾ cups mozzarella cheese, cut into
   small dice
32 black olives, pitted and halved
3 tbsp chopped fresh parsley
serves 4

1 Preheat the oven to 475°F for at least 20 minutes before baking the pizza. Heat half the oil in a large frying pan. Add the onions, and cook over low heat until soft, translucent, and beginning to brown, 12–15 minutes. Season with salt and pepper. Remove from the heat.

2 ▲ Spread the onions over the prepared pizza dough in an even layer, leaving the rim uncovered. Sprinkle with the mozzarella.

3 ▲ Dot with the olives. Sprinkle with parsley and the remaining olive oil. Immediately place the pizza in the oven. Bake for about 15–20 minutes, or until the crust is golden brown and the cheese is bubbling.

Pizza with Seafood

Pizza con frutti di mare

Any combination of shellfish or other seafood can be used as a pizza topping.

Ingredients

1lb peeled plum tomatoes, fresh or
    canned, weighed whole, without extra
    juice
6 oz small squid
8 oz fresh mussels
1 recipe Basic Pizza Dough, rolled out
6 oz shrimp, raw or cooked, peeled and
    deveined
2 cloves garlic, finely chopped
3 tbsp chopped fresh parsley
salt and freshly ground black pepper
3 tbsp olive oil

serves 4

1 ▲ Preheat the oven to 475°F for at least 20 minutes before baking the pizza. Strain the tomatoes through the medium holes of a food mill placed over a bowl, scraping in all the pulp.

2 ▲ Working near the sink, clean the squid by first peeling off the thin skin from the body section. Rinse well. Pull the head and tentacles away from the sac section. Some of the intestines will come away with the head.

3 ▲ Remove and discard the translucent quill and any remaining insides from the sac. Sever the tentacles from the head. Discard the head and intestines. Remove the small hard beak from the base of the tentacles. Rinse the sac and tentacles under running water. Drain. Slice the sacs into rings ¼ in thick.

4 ▲ Scrape any barnacles off the mussels, and scrub well with a stiff brush. Rinse in several changes of cold water. Place the mussels in a saucepan and heat until they open. Lift them out with a slotted spoon, and remove to a side dish. (Discard any that do not open.) Break off the empty half shells, and discard.

5 ▲ Spread some of the puréed tomatoes on the prepared pizza dough, leaving the rim uncovered. Dot evenly with the shrimp and squid rings and tentacles. Sprinkle with the garlic, parsley, salt and pepper, and olive oil. Immediately place the pizza in the oven. Bake for about 8 minutes.

6 ▲ Remove from the oven, and add the mussels in the half shells. Return to the oven and bake for 7–10 minutes more, or until the crust is golden.

~ VARIATION ~

Fresh clams may be added: scrub them well under cold running water. Place in a saucepan and heat until the shells open. Lift them out and remove to a side dish. Discard any that do not open. Break off the empty half shells, and discard. Add to the pizza after 8 minutes of baking.

Pizza with Herbs

Pizza in bianco con erbe aromatiche

This simple topping of mixed fresh herbs, olive oil and salt make a delicious hot pizza which can also be eaten as a bread. In Italy it is often served in a pizzeria and eaten as an appetizer.

Ingredients
1 recipe Basic Pizza Dough, rolled out
4 tbsp chopped mixed fresh herbs, such as thyme, rosemary, basil, parsley or sage
salt, to taste
6 tbsp extra-virgin olive oil
serves 4

1 ▲ Preheat the oven to 475°F for at least 20 minutes before baking the pizza. Sprinkle the prepared dough with the herbs, and salt.

2 ▲ Sprinkle with olive oil. Immediately place the pizza in the oven. Bake for about 20 minutes, or until the crust is golden brown.

Sicilian Closed Pizza

Sfinciuni

These can be stuffed with any pizza topping.

Ingredients
1 recipe Basic Pizza Dough, risen once
2 tbsp coarse cornmeal
3 hard-boiled eggs, peeled and sliced
¼ cup anchovy fillets, drained and chopped
12 olives, pitted
8 leaves fresh basil, torn into pieces
6 medium tomatoes, peeled, seeded and diced
2 cloves garlic, finely chopped
freshly ground black pepper
1½ cups grated caciocavallo or pecorino cheese
olive oil, for brushing
serves 4–6

1 Preheat the oven to 450°F. Punch the dough and knead lightly for 3–4 minutes. Divide the dough into two pieces, one slightly larger than the other. Lightly oil a round pizza pan 15 inches in diameter. Sprinkle with the cornmeal. Roll or press the larger piece of dough into a round slightly bigger than the pan.

2 ▲ Transfer to the pan, bringing the dough up the sides of the pan to the rim. Fill the pie by placing the sliced eggs in the bottom in a layer, leaving the edges of the dough uncovered. Dot with the anchovies, olives and basil.

3 Spread the diced tomatoes over the other ingredients. Sprinkle with garlic and pepper. Top with the grated cheese.

4 ▲ Roll or press the other piece of dough into a circle the same size as the pan. Place it over the filling. Roll the edge of the bottom dough over it, and crimp together to make a border.

5 Brush the top and edges of the pie with olive oil. Bake for 30–40 minutes, or until the top is golden brown. Allow to stand for 5–8 minutes before slicing into wedges.

Calzone

Calzone

A calzone is a pizza folded over to enclose its filling. It can be made large or small, and stuffed with any of the flat pizza fillings. Calzone can be eaten hot or cold.

Ingredients
1 recipe Basic Pizza Dough, risen once
1½ cups ricotta cheese
¾ cup ham, cut into small dice
6 medium tomatoes, peeled, seeded and diced
8 leaves fresh basil, torn into pieces
1 cup mozzarella cheese, cut into small dice
4 tbsp freshly grated Parmesan or Romano cheese
salt and freshly ground black pepper
olive oil, for brushing
serves 4

3 ▲ Combine all the filling ingredients in a bowl, and mix well. Season with salt and pepper.

5 ▲ Fold the other half of the circle over. Crimp the edges of the dough together with your fingers to seal.

1 ▲ Preheat the oven to 475°F for at least 20 minutes before baking the calzone. Punch the dough down and knead it lightly. Divide the dough into 4 balls.

4 ▲ Divide the filling between the 4 circles of dough, placing it on half of each circle and allowing a border of 1 in all around.

6 ▲ Place the calzone on lightly oiled cookie sheets. Brush the tops lightly with olive oil. Bake in the preheated oven for about 15–20 minutes, or until the tops are golden brown and the dough is puffed.

2 ▲ Roll each ball out into a flat circle about ¼ inch thick.

~ COOK'S TIP ~

The calzone is a speciality of Naples. Calzone means "trouser leg" in Italian. This pizza was so named because it resembled a leg of the baggy trousers worn by Neapolitan men in the 18th and 19th centuries. Calzone are now usually round but were originally made from rectangular pieces of dough folded over a long central filling.

Focaccia

Focaccia is an antique form of flat bread which is oiled before baking. It is usually made in a large cookie sheet, and sold in bakeries cut into squares.

Ingredients
1 recipe Basic Pizza Dough, risen once
3 tbsp olive oil
coarse sea salt
serves 6–8 as a side dish

1 ▲ After punching the dough down, knead it for 3–4 minutes. Brush a large shallow baking pan with 1 tbsp of oil.

2 ▲ Place the dough in the pan, and use your fingers to press it into an even layer 1 in thick. Cover the dough with a cloth, and leave to rise in a warm place for 30 minutes. Preheat the oven to 400°F.

~ COOK'S TIP ~

To freeze, allow to cool to room temperature after baking. Wrap in foil and freeze. Thaw and place in a warm oven before serving.

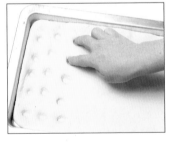

3 ▲ Just before baking, use your fingers to press rows of light indentations into the surface of the focaccia dough.

4 ▲ Brush with the remaining oil, and sprinkle lightly with coarse salt. Bake for about 25 minutes, or until just golden. Cut into squares or wedges and serve as an accompaniment to a meal, or alone, warm or at room temperature.

Focaccia with Onions

Focaccia con cipolle

This appetizing flat bread has a topping of sautéed onions. It can be split and filled with prosciutto or cheese for an unusual sandwich.

Ingredients
1 recipe Basic Pizza Dough, risen once
5 tbsp olive oil
1 medium onion, sliced very thinly and cut
    into short lengths
½ tsp fresh thyme leaves
coarse sea salt
serves 6–8 as a side dish

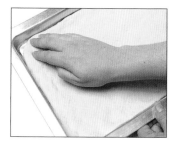

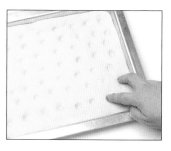

3 ▲ Just before baking, use your fingers to press rows of light indentations into the surface of the focaccia. Brush with the remaining oil.

4 ▲ Spread the onions evenly over the top, and sprinkle lightly with coarse salt. Bake for about 25 minutes, or until just golden. Cut into squares or wedges and serve as an accompaniment to a meal, or alone, warm or at room temperature.

1 ▲ After punching the dough down, knead it for 3–4 minutes. Brush a large shallow baking pan with 1 tbsp of the oil. Place the dough in the pan, and use your fingers to press it into an even layer 1 inch thick. Cover the dough with a cloth, and leave to rise in a warm place for 30 minutes. Preheat the oven to 400°F for 30 minutes during this time.

2 ▲ While the focaccia is rising, heat 3 tbsp of the oil in a medium frying pan. Add the onion, and cook over low heat until soft. Stir in the thyme.

Focaccia with Olives

Focaccia con olive

For this topping, pieces of pitted green olives are pressed onto the dough before baking.

Ingredients
1 recipe Basic Pizza Dough, risen once
3 tbsp olive oil
10–12 large green olives, pitted and cut in
    half lengthwise
coarse sea salt
serves 6–8 as a side dish

1 After punching the dough down, knead it for 3–4 minutes. Brush a large shallow baking pan with 1 tbsp of the oil. Place the dough in the pan, and use your fingers to press it into an even layer 1 inch thick. Cover the dough with a cloth, and leave to rise in a warm place for 30 minutes. Preheat the oven to 400°F for 30 minutes during this time.

2 ▲ Just before baking, use your fingers to press rows of light indentations into the surface of the focaccia. Brush with the remaining oil.

3 ▲ Dot evenly with the olive pieces, and sprinkle with a little coarse salt. Bake for about 25 minutes, or until just golden. Cut into squares or wedges and serve as an accompaniment to a meal, or alone, warm or at room temperature.

Focaccia with Rosemary

Focaccia con rosmarino

One of the most popular breads. If possible, use fresh rosemary for this recipe.

Ingredients
1 recipe Basic Pizza Dough, risen once
3 tbsp olive oil
2 medium sprigs fresh rosemary, coarse
    stalks removed
coarse sea salt
serves 6–8 as a side dish

2 ▲ Scatter with the rosemary leaves. Cover the dough with a cloth, and leave to rise in a warm place for 30 minutes. Preheat the oven to 400°F for 30 minutes during this time.

3 ▲ Just before baking, use your fingers to press rows of light indentations into the surface of the focaccia. Brush with the remaining oil, and sprinkle lightly with coarse salt. Bake for about 25 minutes, or until just golden. Cut into squares or wedges and serve as an accompaniment to a meal, or alone, warm or at room temperature.

1 ▲ After punching the dough down, knead it for 3–4 minutes. Brush a large shallow baking pan with 1 tbsp of the oil. Place the dough in the pan, and use your fingers to press it into an even layer 1 inch thick.

Italian Bread Sticks

Grissini

These typically Italian bread sticks are especially delicious when hand-made. They are still sold loose in many bakeries in Turin and the north of Italy.

Ingredients

1 tbsp fresh cake yeast or ⅓ package
    active dried yeast
½ cup lukewarm water
pinch of sugar
2 tsp malt extract (optional)
1 tsp salt
1¾–2 cups white unbleached flour
makes about 30

1 ▲ Warm a medium mixing bowl by swirling some hot water in it. Drain. Place the yeast in the bowl, and pour on the warm water. Stir in the sugar, mix with a fork, and allow to stand until the yeast has dissolved and starts to foam, 5–10 minutes.

2 ▲ Use a wooden spoon to mix in the malt extract, if using, the salt and about one-third of the flour. Mix in another third of the flour, stirring with the spoon until the dough forms a mass and begins to pull away from the sides of the bowl.

3 ▲ Sprinkle some of the remaining flour onto a smooth work surface. Remove all of the dough from the bowl, and begin to knead it, working in the remaining flour a little at a time. Knead for 8–10 minutes. By the end the dough should be elastic and smooth. Form it into a ball.

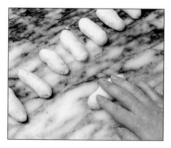

4 ▲ Tear a lump the size of a small walnut from the ball of dough. Roll it lightly between your hands into a small sausage shape. Set it aside on a lightly floured surface. Repeat until all the dough is used up. There should be about 30 pieces.

~ VARIATION ~

Grissini are also good when rolled lightly in poppy or sesame seeds before being baked.

5 ▲ Place one piece of dough on a clean smooth work surface without any flour on it. Roll the dough under the spread-out fingers of both hands, moving your hands backwards and forwards to lengthen and thin the dough into a long strand about ⅜ inch thick. Transfer to a very lightly greased cookie sheet. Repeat with the remaining dough pieces, taking care to roll all the grissini to about the same thickness.

6 ▲ Preheat the oven to 400°F. Cover the tray with a cloth, and place the grissini in a warm place to rise for 10–15 minutes while the oven is heating. Bake for about 8–10 minutes. Remove from the oven. Turn the grissini over, and return them to the oven for 6–7 minutes more. Do not let them brown. Allow to cool. Grissini should be crisp when served. If they lose their crispness on a damp day, warm them in a moderate oven for a few minutes before serving.

Bread with Grapes

Schiacciata con uva

This bread is made to celebrate the grape harvest in central Italy. Use small black grapes with or without seeds; in Italy wine grapes are used.

Ingredients
1½ lb small black grapes
½ cup sugar
1 recipe Basic Pizza Dough, risen once
2 tbsp olive oil
serves 6–8

1 ▲ Remove the grapes from their stems. Wash them well, and pat dry with paper towels. Place in a bowl and sprinkle with the sugar. Set aside until they are needed.

2 ▲ Knead the dough lightly. Divide it into two halves. Roll out or press one half into a circle about ½ inch thick. Place on a lightly oiled flat cookie sheet. Sprinkle with half of the sugared grapes.

3 ▲ Roll out or press the second half of the dough into a circle the same size as the first. Place it on top of the first.

4 ▲ Crimp the edges together. Sprinkle the top with the remaining grapes. Cover the dough with a dish towel and leave in a warm place to rise for 30 minutes. Preheat the oven to 375°F. Sprinkle the bread with the oil, and bake for 50–60 minutes. Allow to cool before cutting into wedges.

Tomato and Basil Tart

Torta di pomodoro e basilico

This tart is similar to a pizza, but uses shortcrust pastry instead of yeast dough for the base.

Ingredients
1½ cups white unbleached flour
½ tsp salt, plus more to sprinkle
½ cup butter or margarine, chilled
3–5 tbsp cold water
2 tbsp extra-virgin olive oil

For the filling
1 cup mozzarella cheese, sliced as thinly
   as possible
12 leaves fresh basil
4–5 medium tomatoes, cut into ¼ inch
   slices
salt and freshly ground black pepper
4 tbsp freshly grated Parmesan cheese
serves 6–8

4 ▲ Line the pastry with a sheet of parchment paper. Fill with dried beans. Place the pie pan on a cookie sheet and bake about 15 minutes. Remove from the oven.

5 Remove the weights and paper. Brush the pastry with oil. Line with the mozzarella. Tear half of the basil into pieces, and sprinkle on top.

6 ▲ Arrange the tomato slices over the cheese. Dot with the remaining whole basil leaves. Sprinkle with salt and pepper, Parmesan and oil. Bake for about 35 minutes. If the cheese exudes a lot of liquid during baking, tilt the pan and spoon it off to keep the pastry from becoming soggy. Serve hot or at room temperature.

1 ▲ Make the pastry by placing the flour and salt in a mixing bowl. Using a pastry blender, cut the butter or margarine into the dry ingredients until the mixture resembles coarse meal. Add 3 tbsp of water, and combine with a fork until the dough holds together. If it is too crumbly, mix in a little more water.

2 Gather the dough into a ball and flatten it into a disc. Wrap in waxed paper and refrigerate for at least 40 minutes. Preheat the oven to 375°F.

3 Roll the pastry out between two sheets of waxed paper to a thickness of ¼ inch. Line an 11 in tart or pie pan, trimming the edges evenly. Refrigerate for 20 minutes. Prick the bottom all over with a fork.

Potato Pizza

Pizza di patate

This "pizza" made of mashed potatoes with a filling of anchovies, capers and tomatoes, is a speciality of Puglia.

Ingredients
2 lb potatoes, scrubbed
½ cup extra-virgin olive oil
salt and freshly ground black pepper
2 cloves garlic, finely chopped
12 oz tomatoes, diced
3 anchovy fillets, chopped
2 tbsp capers, rinsed
serves 4

2 Heat another 3 tbsp of the oil in a medium saucepan. Add the garlic and the chopped tomatoes, and cook over moderate heat until the tomatoes soften and begin to dry out, 12–15 minutes. Meanwhile, preheat the oven to 400°F.

1 ▲ Boil the potatoes in their skins until tender. Peel and mash or pass through a food mill. Beat in 3 tbsp of the oil, and season.

3 ▲ Oil a shallow baking dish. Spread half the mashed potatoes into the dish in an even layer. Cover with the tomatoes, and dot with the chopped anchovies and the capers.

4 ▲ Spread the rest of the potatoes in a layer on top of the filling. Brush the top with the remaining oil. Bake in the preheated oven for 20–25 minutes, or until the top is golden brown. Serve hot, directly from the baking dish.

Bruschetta with Tomato

Bruschetta con pomodoro

Bruschetta is toasted or broiled bread, rubbed with garlic and sprinkled with olive oil or chopped fresh tomatoes. It is eaten as an appetizer or accompaniment.

Ingredients
3–4 medium tomatoes, chopped
salt and freshly ground black pepper
a few leaves fresh basil, torn into pieces
8 slices crusty white bread
2–3 cloves garlic, peeled and cut in half
6 tbsp extra-virgin olive oil
serves 4

1 Place the chopped tomatoes with their juice in a small bowl. Season with salt and pepper, and stir in the basil. Allow to stand for 10 minutes.

2 ▲ Toast or broil the bread until it is crisp on both sides. Rub one side of each piece of toast with the cut garlic.

3 ▲ Arrange on a platter. Sprinkle with the olive oil. Spoon on the chopped tomatoes, and serve at once.

FISH AND SHELLFISH

Garlic, herbs and olive oil transform both sea and freshwater fish, giving them a true Mediterranean taste. Succulent shellfish, enhanced with aromatic seasonings, evoke the summer pleasures of sea and sun.

Stewed Mussels and Clams

Zuppa di cozze e vongole

Casseroles of mixed shellfish are very popular on the Ligurian coast.

Ingredients
1½ lb fresh mussels, in their shells
1½ lb fresh clams, in their shells
5 tbsp olive oil
3 cloves garlic, peeled and crushed
1¼ cups dry white wine
5 tbsp chopped fresh parsley
freshly ground black pepper
rounds of crusty bread, toasted, to serve
serves 4

1 Cut off the "beards" from the mussels. Scrub and rinse the mussels and clams in cold water. Discard any with broken shells.

2 Heat the oil in a large saucepan with the garlic. As soon as this is golden, add the mussels, clams and the wine. Cover, and steam until all the shells have opened, about 5–8 minutes. (Discard any that do not open.)

3 Lift the clams and mussels out, pouring any liquid in the shells back into the saucepan. Place in a warmed serving bowl. Discard the garlic.

4 ▲ Strain the liquid in the saucepan through a layer of paper towels held in a sieve, pouring it over the clams and mussels in the bowl. Sprinkle with parsley and black pepper.

5 ▲ To serve, place rounds of toasted bread in the bottom of individual soup bowls, and ladle in the mussels and clams with some of the hot liquid.

Broiled Shrimp with Herbs

Gamberi con erbe aromatiche

Large shrimp are delicious marinated with fresh herbs, lemon and garlic. They can be broiled or grilled on a barbecue.

Ingredients
24 large raw shrimp, in their shells
3 cloves garlic, finely chopped
3 tbsp finely chopped fresh basil
1 tbsp fresh thyme leaves
2 tbsp finely chopped fresh parsley
1 tbsp coarsely crushed black pepper
juice of 1 lemon
4 tbsp olive oil
8 bay leaves
¼ cup salt pork or pancetta, cut into 8
    small squares
serves 4

1 Shell the shrimp and devein them either by using a deveiner, or by making a shallow incision with a small sharp knife down the center of the back to disclose the long black vein. Remove and discard this.

2 ▲ Place the shrimp in a bowl with the garlic, chopped herbs, pepper, lemon juice and olive oil. Mix well, cover, and leave to marinate in the refrigerator for at least 6 hours, or preferably overnight.

3 ▲ Preheat the broiler. Arrange 6 shrimp on each of 4 skewers so that they lie flat, threading a bay leaf and a square of salt pork between every 2 shrimp. Brush with the remaining marinade. Place in one layer under the broiler or on a barbecue. Cook for about 3 minutes. Turn, and cook for 3 minutes more.

Baked Mussels and Potatoes

Cozze in tortiera con patate

This dish originates from Puglia, noted for its imaginative baked casseroles.

Ingredients

1½ lb large mussels, in their shells
8 oz potatoes, unpeeled
5 tbsp olive oil
2 cloves garlic, finely chopped
8 leaves fresh basil, torn into pieces
8 oz tomatoes, peeled and thinly sliced
3 tbsp plain breadcrumbs
freshly ground black pepper
serves 2–3

1 Cut off the "beards" from the mussels. Scrub and soak in several changes of cold water. Discard any with broken shells. Place the mussels with a cupful of water in a large saucepan over moderate heat. As soon as they open, lift them out. Remove and discard the empty half shells, leaving the mussels in the other half. (Discard any mussels that do not open.) Strain any liquid in the pan through a layer of paper towels, and reserve.

2 ▲ Boil the potatoes. Remove them from the water when they are still quite firm and peel and slice them.

3 ▲ Preheat the oven to 350°F. Spread 2 tbsp of the olive oil in the bottom of a shallow ovenproof dish. Cover with the potato slices in one layer. Add the mussels in their half shells in one layer. Sprinkle with garlic and pieces of basil.

4 ▲ Cover with a layer of the tomato slices. Sprinkle with breadcrumbs and black pepper, the filtered mussel liquid and the remaining olive oil. Bake for about 20 minutes, or until the tomatoes are soft and the breadcrumbs golden. Serve directly from the baking dish.

Shrimp in Spicy Tomato Sauce

Gamberi alla marinara

The tomato sauce base can be sharpened up by adding hot chilies.

Ingredients

6 tbsp olive oil
1 medium onion, finely chopped
1 stalk celery, finely chopped
1 small red pepper, seeded and chopped
½ cup red wine
1 tbsp wine vinegar
1 × 14 oz can plum tomatoes, chopped,
    with their juice
salt and freshly ground black pepper
2 lb fresh shrimp, in their shells
2–3 cloves garlic, finely chopped
3 tbsp finely chopped fresh parsley
1 piece dried chili, crumbled or chopped
    (optional)

serves 6

4 ▲ Heat the remaining oil in a clean heavy saucepan. Stir in the garlic, parsley and chili, if using. Cook over moderate heat, stirring constantly, until the garlic is golden. Do not let it brown. Add the tomato sauce and bring to a boil. Taste for seasoning.

5 ▲ Stir in the shrimp. Bring the sauce back to a boil. Reduce the heat slightly and simmer until the shrimp are pink and firm, 4–6 minutes, depending on their size. Remove from the heat and serve.

1 In a heavy saucepan, heat half of the oil. Add the onion, and cook over low heat until soft. Stir in the celery and chopped pepper, and cook for 5 minutes more. Raise the heat to medium high, and add the wine, vinegar and tomatoes. Season with salt and pepper. Bring to a boil and cook for about 5 minutes.

2 ▲ Lower the heat, cover the pan, and simmer until the vegetables are soft, about 30 minutes. Purée the sauce through a food mill.

3 Shell the shrimp and devein them, either by using a deveiner or by making a shallow incision with a small sharp knife down the center of the back to disclose the long black vein. Remove and discard.

roiled Fresh Sardines

Sarde alla griglia

Fresh sardines are flavorful and firm-fleshed, and quite different in taste and consistency from those canned in oil. They are excellent simply broiled and served with lemon.

Ingredients
2 lb very fresh sardines, gutted and with
    heads removed
olive oil, for brushing
salt and freshly ground black pepper
3 tbsp chopped fresh parsley, to serve
lemon wedges, to garnish
serves 4–6

1 Preheat the broiler. Rinse the sardines in water. Pat dry with paper towels.

2 ▲ Brush the sardines lightly with olive oil and sprinkle generously with salt and pepper. Place the sardines in one layer on the broiling pan. Broil for about 3–4 minutes.

3 ▲ Turn, and cook for 3–4 minutes more, or until the skin begins to brown. Serve immediately, sprinkled with parsley and garnished with lemon wedges.

Baked Aromatic Sea Bass

Branzino aromatizzato al forno

Sea bass is a firm white-fleshed fish which benefits from simple cooking. Use fresh herbs for this recipe, if possible.

Ingredients
1 large sea bass, about 3 lb
4 bay leaves
few sprigs fresh thyme
8–10 sprigs fresh parsley
few sprigs fresh fennel, tarragon or basil
1 tbsp peppercorns
9 tbsp extra-virgin olive oil
salt and freshly ground black pepper
flour, for coating
lemon wedges, to garnish
serves 5–6

1 Gut the fish, leaving the head on. Wash carefully in cold water. Pat dry with paper towels. Place half of the herbs and peppercorns in the bottom of a shallow platter, and lay the fish on top of them. Arrange the remaining herbs on top of the fish and in its cavity. Sprinkle with 3 tbsp of the oil. Cover lightly with foil, and place in the refrigerator for 2 hours.

2 ▲ Preheat the oven to 400°F. Remove and discard all the herbs from around the fish. Pat it dry with paper towels. Spread a little flour in a platter and season it with salt and pepper. Roll the fish in the flour, and shake off the excess.

3 ▲ Heat the remaining olive oil in a flameproof dish just large enough to hold the fish comfortably. When the oil is hot, add the fish, and brown it quickly on both sides. Transfer the dish to the oven, and bake for 25–40 minutes, depending on the size of the fish. The fish is cooked when the dorsal fin (in the middle of the backbone) comes out easily when pulled. Serve garnished with lemon wedges.

tuffed Squid

Calamari ripieni

Squid are popular in all the coastal regions of Italy. They are very tender and easy to cook.

Ingredients

2 lb fresh squid (about 16 medium)
juice of ½ lemon
2 anchovy fillets, chopped
2 cloves garlic, finely chopped
3 medium tomatoes, peeled, seeded and
    finely chopped
2 tbsp chopped fresh parsley
½ cup plain breadcrumbs
1 egg
salt and freshly ground black pepper
2 tbsp olive oil
½ cup dry white wine
few sprigs fresh parsley, to garnish
serves 4

1 Working near the sink, clean the squid by first peeling off the thin skin from the body section. Rinse well. Pull the head and tentacles away from the body sac. Some of the intestines will come away with the head. Remove and discard the translucent quill and any remaining insides from the sac. Sever the tentacles from the head. Discard the head and intestines.

2 Remove and discard the small hard beak from the base of the tentacles. Place the tentacles in a bowl of water with the lemon juice. Rinse the sacs well under cold running water. Pat the insides dry with paper towels.

3 ▲ Preheat the oven to 350°F. Drain the tentacles. Chop them coarsely and place in a mixing bowl. Stir in the next 6 ingredients and season. Use this mixture to loosely stuff the squid sacs. Close the opening to the sacs with wooden toothpicks.

4 ▲ Oil a shallow baking dish large enough to accommodate the squid in one layer. Arrange the squid sacs in the dish. Pour over the oil and wine. Bake uncovered for 35–45 minutes, or until tender. Remove the toothpicks and serve garnished with parsley.

~ COOK'S TIP ~

Do not overstuff the squid sacs or they may burst during cooking.

Deep-fried Shrimp and Squid

Fritto misto

The Italian name of this recipe means "mixed fry". Any mixture of seafood can be used.

Ingredients

vegetable oil, for deep-frying
1¼ lb medium-sized fresh shrimp,
    shelled and deveined
1¼ lb squid (about 12 medium) cleaned
    and cut into bite-size pieces
1 cup flour
lemon wedges, to serve

For the batter

2 egg whites
2 tbsp olive oil
1 tbsp white wine vinegar
scant 1 cup flour
2 tsp baking soda
⅓ cup cornstarch
salt and freshly ground black pepper
1 cup water
serves 6

1 Make the batter in a large bowl by beating the egg whites, olive oil and vinegar together lightly with a wire whisk. Beat in the dry ingredients, and whisk until well blended. Beat in the water, a little at a time. Cover the bowl, and allow to stand 15 minutes.

2 Heat the oil for deep-frying until a small piece of bread sizzles as soon as it is dropped in (about 360°F).

3 Dredge the shrimp and squid pieces in the flour, shaking off any excess. Dip them quickly into the batter. Fry in small batches for about 1 minute, stirring with a slotted spoon to keep them from sticking to each other.

4 ▲ Remove and drain on paper towels. Allow the oil to come back up to the correct temperature between batches. Sprinkle lightly with salt, and serve hot with lemon wedges.

eafood Stew

Zuppa di pesce

"Soups" – really stews – of mixed fish and shellfish are specialities of the Mediterranean.

Ingredients

3 tbsp olive oil
1 medium onion, sliced
1 carrot, sliced
½ stalk celery, sliced
2 cloves garlic, chopped
1 × 14 oz can plum tomatoes, chopped, with their juice
8 oz fresh shrimp, peeled and deveined (reserve the shells)
1 lb white fish bones and heads, gills removed
1 bay leaf
1 sprig fresh thyme, or ¼ tsp dried thyme leaves
a few peppercorns
salt and freshly ground black pepper
1½ lb fresh mussels, in their shells, scrubbed and rinsed
1 lb fresh small clams, in their shells, scrubbed and rinsed
1 cup white wine
2 lb mixed fish fillets, such as cod, monkfish, red snapper or hake, bones removed and cut into chunks
3 tbsp finely chopped fresh parsley
rounds of French bread, toasted, to serve

serves 6–8

2 ▲ Place the shrimp shells in a large saucepan with the fish bones and heads. Add the herbs and peppercorns, and pour in 3 cups of water. Bring to a boil, reduce the heat, and simmer for 25 minutes, skimming off any scum that rises to the surface. Strain and pour into a pan with the tomato sauce. Season to taste.

3 Place the mussels and clams in a saucepan with the wine. Cover, and steam until all the shells have opened. (Discard any that do not open.)

4 Lift the clams and mussels out and set aside. Filter the cooking liquid through a layer of paper towel and add it to the stock and tomato sauce. Check the seasoning.

5 ▲ Bring the sauce to a boil. Add the fish, and boil for 5 minutes. Add the shrimp and boil for 3–4 minutes. Stir in the mussels and clams and cook for 2–3 minutes more. Transfer the stew to a warmed casserole. Sprinkle with parsley, and serve with the toasted rounds of French bread.

1 ▲ Heat the oil in a medium saucepan. Add the onion, and cook slowly until soft. Stir in the carrot and celery, and cook for 5 minutes more. Add the garlic, the tomatoes and their juice, and 1 cup of water. Cook over moderate heat until the vegetables are soft, about 15 minutes. Purée in a food processor or pass through a food mill. Set aside.

Trout Baked in Paper with Olives   *Trota in cartoccio con olive*

Baking fish in paper packets keeps in all the flavor and moisture.

Ingredients

4 medium trout, about 10 oz each, gutted
5 tbsp olive oil
4 bay leaves
salt and freshly ground black pepper
4 slices pancetta or bacon
4 tbsp chopped shallots
4 tbsp chopped fresh parsley
½ cup dry white wine
24 green olives, pitted
serves 4

1 ▲ Preheat the oven to 400°F. Wash the trout well in cold running water. Drain. Pat dry with paper towels.

2 ▲ Lightly brush oil onto 4 pieces of parchment paper each large enough to enclose one fish. Lay one fish on each piece of oiled paper. Place a bay leaf in each cavity, and sprinkle with salt and pepper.

3 ▲ Wrap a slice of pancetta around each fish. Sprinkle with 1 tbsp each of chopped shallots and parsley. Drizzle each fish with 1 tbsp of oil and 2 tbsp of white wine. Add 6 olives to each packet.

4 ▲ Close the paper loosely around the fish, rolling the edges together to seal them completely. Bake for 20–25 minutes. Place each packet on an individual plate and open at the table.

oiled Salmon Steaks with Fennel   *Salmone alla griglia*

nnel grows wild all over the south of Italy. Its mild aniseed flavor goes well with fish.

ngredients
juice of 1 lemon
3 tbsp chopped fresh fennel herb, or the
    green fronds from the top of a fennel
    bulb
1 tsp fennel seeds
3 tbsp olive oil
4 salmon steaks of the same thickness,
    about 1½ lb total
salt and freshly ground black pepper
lemon wedges, to garnish
serves 4

1 Combine the lemon juice, chopped
fennel and fennel seeds with the olive
oil in a bowl. Add the salmon steaks,
turning them to coat them with the
marinade. Sprinkle with salt and pepper.
Cover and place in the refrigerator.
Allow to stand for 2 hours.

2 ▲ Preheat the broiler. Arrange the
fish in one layer on a broiling pan or
cookie sheet. Broil about 4 in from the
heat source for 3–4 minutes.

3 ▲ Turn. Spoon on the remaining
marinade and broil for 3–4 minutes on
the other side, or until the edges begin
to brown. Serve hot garnished with
lemon wedges.

Octopus with Lemon and Garlic   *Polpo con limone e aglio*

Octopus is widely appreciated in Italy. Dressed with oil and lemon it is delicious.

Ingredients
2 lb octopus (young and small
    if possible)
2 tbsp chopped fresh parsley
2 cloves garlic, very finely chopped
4 tbsp extra-virgin olive oil
3 tbsp fresh lemon juice
freshly ground black pepper
serves 3–4

1 Beat the octopus repeatedly against
a strong table or marble surface. Clean,
removing the eyes, beak and sacs. (Or
ask your fishmonger to do this.) Wash
carefully under cold running water.

2 Place the octopus in a large
saucepan with cold water to cover.
Bring to a boil, cover the pan tightly,
and simmer gently until tender, 45
minutes for small octopus and up to 2
hours for larger ones. Skim off any
cum which rises to the surface.

3 ▲ Remove from the pan, and allow
to cool slightly. Rub the octopus lightly
with a clean cloth to remove any loose
dark skin. Slice the warm octopus into
rounds ¾ inch wide.

~ COOK'S TIP ~

In Italy, a wine cork is placed in
the saucepan with the octopus
to reduce the scum.

4 ▲ Place the octopus pieces in a
serving bowl. Toss with the parsley,
garlic, olive oil and lemon juice.
Sprinkle with pepper. Mix well. Allow
to stand for at least 20 minutes before
serving at room temperature.

ked Cod with Garlic Mayonnaise

Merluzzo al forno

though cod is not native to the Mediterranean, a similar species is used for this dish.

ngredients

4 anchovy fillets
3 tbsp chopped fresh parsley
coarsely ground black pepper
6 tbsp olive oil
4 cod fillets, about 1½ lb total, skinned
⅓ cup plain breadcrumbs

For the mayonnaise

2 cloves garlic, finely chopped
1 egg yolk
1 tsp Dijon mustard
¾ cup vegetable oil
salt and freshly ground black pepper

serves 4

1 Make the mayonnaise. First put the garlic in a mortar or small bowl. Mash it to a paste. Beat in the egg yolk and mustard. Add the oil in a thin stream while beating vigorously with a small wire whisk. When the mixture is thick and smooth, season with salt and pepper. Cover the bowl and keep cool.

2 ▲ Preheat the oven to 400°F. Chop the anchovy fillets with the parsley very finely. Place in a small bowl, and add pepper and 3 tbsp of the oil. Stir to a paste.

3 ▲ Place the cod fillets in one layer in an oiled baking dish. Spread the anchovy paste on the top of the cod fillets. Sprinkle with the breadcrumbs and the remaining oil. Bake for 20–25 minutes, or until the breadcrumbs are golden. Serve hot with the garlic mayonnaise.

Monkfish Medallions with Thyme

Pescatrice con timo

Monkfish has a sweet flesh that combines well with Mediterranean flavors.

Ingredients

1¼ lb monkfish fillet, preferably in one piece
3 tbsp extra-virgin olive oil
½ cup small black olives, preferably from the Riviera, pitted
1 large or 2 small tomatoes, seeded and diced
1 sprig fresh thyme, or 1 tsp dried thyme leaves
salt and freshly ground black pepper
1 tbsp very finely chopped fresh parsley, to serve

serves 4

1 Preheat the oven to 400°F. Remove he grey membrane from the onkfish, if necessary. Cut the fish slices ½ in thick.

2 Heat a non-stick frying pan quite hot, without oil. Sear the fish quickly on both sides. Remove to a side dish.

3 ▲ Spread 1 tbsp of the olive oil in the bottom of a shallow baking dish. Arrange the fish in one layer. Distribute the olives and diced tomato on top of the fish.

4 Sprinkle the fish with thyme, salt and pepper, and the remaining oil. Bake for 10–12 minutes.

5 ▲ To serve, divide the medallions between 4 warmed plates. Spoon on the vegetables and any cooking juices. Sprinkle with the chopped parsley.

Stuffed Swordfish Rolls

Involtini di pesce spada

Swordfish is abundant around Sicily and it features in many dishes.

Ingredients

4 slices fresh swordfish about
    ½ in thick
6 tbsp olive oil
1 clove garlic, finely chopped (optional)
½ cup plain breadcrumbs
2 tbsp capers, rinsed, drained and
    chopped
10 leaves fresh basil, chopped
4 tbsp fresh lemon juice
salt and freshly ground black pepper
For the tomato sauce
2 tbsp olive oil
1 clove garlic, peeled and crushed
1 small onion, finely chopped
1 lb tomatoes, peeled
½ cup dry white wine
salt and freshly ground black pepper
serves 4

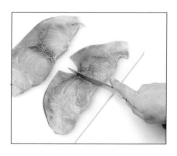

1 ▲ Cut the swordfish slices in half, removing any bones. Brush with 2 tbsp of the olive oil, and refrigerate until needed.

2 Make the tomato sauce by heating the oil in a medium heavy saucepan. Add the garlic, and cook until golden. Discard the garlic. Add the onion, and cook over low heat until soft. Stir in the tomatoes and wine. Season with salt and pepper. Cover the pan, and cook over moderate heat for 15 minutes. Pass the sauce through a food mill or purée in a food processor. Season, and keep warm while you prepare the fish. Preheat the oven to 400°F.

3 In a small bowl combine 2 tbsp of olive oil with the garlic if using, breadcrumbs, capers, basil and lemon juice. Season with salt and pepper and mix to a paste.

4 ▲ Lay the swordfish slices out flat on a board. Divide the stuffing between the slices and spread it over the center of each. Roll the slices and secure with wooden toothpicks.

5 ▲ Heat the remaining oil in a flameproof dish. Add the swordfish rolls and brown them quickly over high heat, turning them once or twice. After 3–4 minutes pour in the tomato sauce. Place the dish in the oven, and bake for 15 minutes, basting occasionally. Serve warm.

Red Mullet with Tomatoes

Triglie con pomodoro

Red mullet is a popular fish in Italy, and this recipe accentuates both its flavor and color.

Ingredients

4 red mullet or red snapper, about 6–7 oz
  each
1 lb tomatoes, peeled, or 1 × 14 oz can
  plum tomatoes
4 tbsp olive oil
4 tbsp finely chopped fresh parsley
2 cloves garlic, finely chopped
salt and freshly ground black pepper
½ cup white wine
4 thin lemon slices, cut in half
serves 4

1 ▲ Scale and clean the fish without removing the liver. Wash and pat dry with paper towels.

2 ▲ Chop the tomatoes into small pieces. Heat the oil in a saucepan or casserole large enough to hold the fish in one layer. Add the parsley and garlic, and sauté for 1 minute. Stir in the tomatoes and cook over moderate heat for 15–20 minutes. Season with salt and pepper.

3 ▲ Add the fish to the tomato sauce and cook over moderate to high heat for 5 minutes. Add the wine and the lemon slices. Bring the sauce back to a boil, and cook for about 5 minutes more. Turn the fish over, and cook for 4–5 minutes more. Remove the fish to a warmed serving platter and keep warm until needed.

4 ▲ Boil the sauce for 3–4 minutes to reduce it slightly. Spoon it over the fish, and serve.

~ VARIATION ~

Small sea bass may be substituted.

Sole with Sweet and Sour Sauce

Sfogi in saor

This Venetian dish should be prepared 1–2 days before it is to be eaten.

Ingredients
3–4 fillets of sole, about 1¼ lb total, divided in half
4 tbsp flour
salt and freshly ground black pepper
pinch of ground cloves
6–8 tbsp olive oil
generous ¼ cup pine nuts
3 bay leaves
pinch of ground cinnamon
pinch of grated nutmeg
4 cloves
1 small onion, very finely sliced
¼ cup dry white wine
¼ cup white wine vinegar
⅓ cup sultanas
serves 4

1 Dredge the sole fillets in the flour seasoned with salt and pepper and the ground cloves.

2 Heat 3 tbsp of the oil in a heavy frying pan or skillet. Cook the sole fillets a few at a time until golden, about 3 minutes on each side. Add more oil as necessary.

3 ▲ Remove with a slotted spatula to a large shallow serving dish. Sprinkle with the pine nuts, bay leaves, cinnamon, nutmeg and whole cloves.

4 ▲ Heat the remaining oil in a saucepan. Add the onion, and cook over low heat until golden. Add the wine, vinegar and sultanas, and boil for 4–5 minutes. Pour over the fish. Cover the dish with foil, and leave in a cool place for 24–48 hours. Remove 2 hours before serving. This dish is traditionally eaten at room temperature.

Salt Cod with Parsley and Garlic

Baccalà alla bolognese

Salt cod is very popular all over Italy. For centuries it has been imported from Scandinavia.
The very salty fish must be soaked for 24 hours in water to reduce its salt content.

Ingredients
1½ lb boneless and skinless salt cod, preferably in one piece
flour seasoned with freshly ground black pepper, for dredging
2 tbsp extra-virgin olive oil
3 tbsp finely chopped fresh parsley
2 cloves garlic, finely chopped
2 tbsp butter, cut into small pieces
lemon wedges, to serve
serves 4–5

1 Cut the salt cod into 2 in squares. Place them in a large bowl and cover with cold water. Allow to stand for at least 24 hours, changing the water frequently.

2 ▲ Preheat the oven to 375°F. Drain the fish, shaking out the excess moisture. Remove any remaining bones or skin. Dredge lightly in the seasoned flour.

3 Spread 1 tbsp of the oil over the bottom of a baking dish large enough to hold the fish in one layer.

4 ▲ Place the fish in the dish. Combine the chopped parsley and garlic, and sprinkle evenly over the fish. Sprinkle with the remaining oil, and dot with butter. Bake for 15 minutes. Turn the fish, and bake for 15–20 minutes more, or until tender. Serve at once, with the lemon wedges.

MEAT, POULTRY AND GAME

From the Florentine simplicity of Chicken Breasts Cooked in Butter to the more complex flavors of Lamb Stewed with Tomatoes and Garlic, this chapter presents the highlights of classic Italian cuisine.

Chicken with Peppers

Pollo con peperoni

This colorful dish comes from the south of Italy, where sweet peppers are plentiful.

Ingredients
3 lb chicken, cut into serving pieces
3 large peppers, red, yellow, or green
6 tbsp olive oil
2 medium red onions, finely sliced
2 cloves garlic, finely chopped
small piece of dried chili, crumbled
    (optional)
½ cup white wine
salt and freshly ground black pepper
2 tomatoes, fresh or canned, peeled and
    chopped
3 tbsp chopped fresh parsley
serves 4

1 Trim any fat off the chicken, and remove all excess skin. Wash the peppers. Prepare by cutting them in half, scooping out the seeds, and cutting away the stem. Slice into strips.

2 ▲ Heat half the oil in a large heavy saucepan or casserole. Add the onion, and cook over low heat until soft. Remove to a side dish. Add the remaining oil to the pan, raise the heat to moderate, add the chicken and brown on all sides, 6–8 minutes. Return the onions to the pan, and add the garlic and dried chili, if using.

3 ▲ Pour in the wine, and cook until it has reduced by half. Add the peppers and stir well to coat them with the fats. Season. After 3–4 minutes, stir in the tomatoes. Lower the heat, cover the pan, and cook until the peppers are soft, and the chicken is cooked, about 25–30 minutes. Stir occasionally. Stir in the parsley and serve.

Chicken Breasts Cooked in Butter

Petti di pollo alla fiorentina

This simple and delicious way of cooking chicken brings out all of its delicacy.

Ingredients
4 small chicken breasts, skinned and
    boned
flour seasoned with salt and freshly
    ground black pepper, for dredging
⅓ cup butter
1 sprig fresh parsley, to garnish
serves 4

1 Separate the two fillets of each breast. They come apart very easily; one is large, the other small. Pound the large fillets lightly to flatten them. Dredge the chicken in the seasoned flour, shaking off any excess.

~ COOK'S TIP ~

This chicken dish should be accompanied by delicately flavored vegetables so that its subtle taste is not overpowered.

2 ▲ Heat the butter in a large heavy frying pan until it bubbles. Place all the chicken fillets in the pan, in one layer if possible. Cook over moderate to high heat for 3–4 minutes until they are golden brown.

3 ▲ Turn the chicken over. Reduce the heat to low to moderate, and continue cooking until the fillets are cooked through but still springy to the touch, about 9–12 minutes in all. If the chicken begins to brown too much, cover the pan for the final minutes of cooking. Serve at once garnished with a little parsley.

Roast Chicken with Fennel

Pollo con finocchio

In Italy this dish is prepared with wild fennel. Cultivated fennel bulb works just as well.

Ingredients
3½ lb roasting chicken
salt and freshly ground black pepper
1 onion, quartered
½ cup olive oil
2 medium fennel bulbs
1 clove garlic, peeled
pinch of grated nutmeg
3–4 thin slices pancetta or bacon
½ cup dry white wine
serves 4–5

1 Preheat the oven to 350°F. Rinse the chicken in cold water. Pat it dry inside and out with paper towels. Sprinkle the cavity with salt and pepper. Place the onion quarters in the cavity. Rub the chicken with about 3 tbsp of the olive oil. Place in a roasting pan.

2 Cut the green fronds from the tops of the fennel bulbs. Chop the fronds with the garlic. Place in a small bowl and mix with the nutmeg. Season with salt and pepper.

3 ▲ Sprinkle the fennel mixture over the chicken, pressing it onto the oiled skin. Cover the breast with the slices of pancetta or bacon. Sprinkle with 2 tbsp of oil. Place in the oven and roast for 30 minutes.

4 Meanwhile, boil or steam the fennel bulbs until barely tender. Remove from the heat and cut into quarters or sixths lengthwise. After the chicken has been cooking for 30 minutes, remove the pan from the oven. Baste the chicken with any oils in the pan.

5 Arrange the fennel pieces around the chicken. Sprinkle the fennel with the remaining oil. Pour about half the wine over the chicken, and return the pan to the oven.

6 ▲ After 30 minutes more, baste the chicken again. Pour on the remaining wine. Cook for 15–20 minutes more. To test, prick the thigh with a fork. If the juices run clear, the chicken is cooked. Transfer the chicken to a serving platter, and arrange the fennel around it.

Chicken with Ham and Cheese

Petti di pollo alla bolognese

This tasty combination comes from Emilia-Romagna, where it is also prepared with veal.

Ingredients
4 small chicken breasts, skinned and
    boned
flour seasoned with salt and freshly
    ground black pepper, for dredging
¼ cup butter
3–4 leaves fresh sage
4 thin slices prosciutto crudo, or cooked
    ham, cut in half
½ cup freshly grated Parmesan or
    Romano cheese
serves 4

1 Cut each breast in half lengthwise to make two flat fillets of approximately the same thickness. Dredge the chicken in the seasoned flour, and shake off the excess.

2 ▲ Preheat the broiler. Heat the butter in a large heavy frying pan or skillet with the sage leaves. Add the chicken in one layer, and cook over low to moderate heat until golden brown on both sides, turning as necessary.

3 ▲ Remove the chicken from the heat, and arrange on a flameproof serving dish or broiling pan. Place one piece of ham on each chicken fillet, and top with the grated Parmesan or Romano. Broil for 3–4 minutes, or until the cheese has melted.

Mediterranean Turkey Skewers

Spiedini di tacchino

These skewers are delicious, and can be cooked under a broiler or on a charcoal barbecue.

Ingredients

6 tbsp olive oil
3 tbsp fresh lemon juice
1 clove garlic, finely chopped
2 tbsp chopped fresh basil
salt and freshly ground black pepper
2 medium zucchini
1 long thin eggplant
11 oz boneless turkey, cut into
    2 in cubes
12–16 pickled onions
1 pepper, red or yellow, cut into 2 in
    squares

serves 4

3 ▲ Prepare the skewers by alternating the turkey, onions, and pepper pieces. Lay the prepared skewers on a platter, and sprinkle with the flavored oil. Leave to marinate for at least 30 minutes. Preheat the broiler, or prepare a barbecue.

4 ▲ Broil for about 10 minutes, or until the vegetables are tender, turning the skewers occasionally. Serve hot.

1 ▲ In a small bowl mix the oil with the lemon juice, garlic and basil. Season with salt and pepper.

2 ▲ Slice the zucchini and eggplant lengthwise into strips ¼ inch thick. Cut them crosswise about two-thirds of the way along their length. Discard the shorter length. Wrap half the turkey pieces with the zucchini slices, and the other half with the eggplant slices.

Turkey Cutlets with Olives   *Petto di tacchino con olive*

This quick and tasty dish makes a good light main course.

Ingredients

6 tbsp olive oil
1 clove garlic, peeled and lightly crushed
1 dried chili, lightly crushed
1¼ lb boneless turkey breast, cut into
 ¼ inch slices
salt and freshly ground black pepper
½ cup dry white wine
4 tomatoes, peeled and seeded, cut into
 thin strips
about 24 black olives
6–8 leaves fresh basil, torn into pieces
serves 4

1 ▲ Heat 4 tbsp of the olive oil in a large frying pan. Add the garlic and dried chili, and cook over low heat until the garlic is golden.

2 ▲ Raise the heat to moderate. Place the turkey slices in the pan, and brown them lightly on both sides. Season with salt and pepper. The turkey will be cooked after about 2 minutes. Remove the turkey to a heated dish.

3 ▲ Discard the garlic and chili. Add the wine, tomato strips and olives. Cook over moderate heat for 3–4 minutes, scraping up any meat residue from the bottom of the pan.

4 ▲ Return the turkey to the pan. Sprinkle with the basil. Heat for about 30 seconds, and serve.

Stuffed Turkey Breast with Lemon *Petto di tacchino ripieno*

This elegant dish of rolled turkey breast makes an impressive but economical main course.

Ingredients

1½ lb turkey breast, in one piece
1 carrot, cut into matchsticks
1 medium zucchini, cut into matchsticks
⅓ cup ham, cut into matchsticks
2 thick slices white bread, crusts
    removed, softened in a little milk
10 green olives, pitted and finely chopped
1 large clove garlic, finely chopped
4 tbsp chopped fresh parsley
4 tbsp finely chopped fresh basil
1 egg
⅛ tsp grated lemon zest
2 tbsp freshly grated Parmesan cheese
salt and freshly ground black pepper
4 tbsp olive oil
1 cup fresh or canned chicken stock,
    warmed
½ lemon, cut into thin wedges
2 tbsp butter
serves 4–5

1 ▲ Remove any bones, skin or fat from the turkey. Using a sharp knife, cut part of the way through the turkey breast and open the two halves out like a book.

~ VARIATION ~

Substitute 3 oz sliced mushrooms sautéed lightly in 3 tbsp butter for the ham in step 3. Omit the lemon wedges during cooking.

2 ▲ Pound the meat with a mallet to obtain one large piece of meat of as even a thickness as possible.

3 ▲ Preheat the oven to 400°F. Blanch the carrot and zucchini pieces in a small saucepan of boiling water for 2 minutes. Drain. Combine with the matchsticks of ham.

4 ▲ Squeeze the bread, and place in a mixing bowl, breaking it into small pieces with a fork. Stir in the olives, garlic and herbs, and the egg. Add the lemon zest and grated Parmesan. Season with salt and pepper.

5 ▲ Spread the bread mixture in one layer over the meat, leaving a small border all around. Cover with the ham and vegetable mixture. Roll the turkey up. Tie the roll in several places with string.

6 ▲ Heat the oil in a flameproof casserole slightly larger than the turkey roll. When the oil is hot, brown the meat on all sides. Remove from the heat, add the stock, and arrange the lemon wedges around the meat. Cover and place in the oven.

7 After 15 minutes remove the cover, discard the lemon and baste the meat. Continue cooking, uncovered, for a further 25–30 minutes, basting occasionally. Allow to stand for at least 10 minutes before slicing.

8 Strain the sauce. Stir in the butter and taste for seasoning. Serve the sliced roll warm with the sauce. If you wish to serve it cold, slice the roll just before serving and omit the sauce.

Pan-Fried Marinated Poussin

Galletti marinati in padella

These small birds are full of flavor when marinated for several hours before cooking.

Ingredients
2 poussins, about 1 lb each
5–6 leaves fresh mint, torn into pieces
1 leek, sliced into thin rings
1 clove garlic, finely chopped
salt and coarsely ground black pepper
4 tbsp olive oil
2 tbsp fresh lemon juice
¼ cup dry white wine
mint leaves, to garnish
serves 3–4

1 Cut the poussins in half down the backbone, dividing the breast. Flatten the 4 halves with a mallet. Place them in a bowl with the mint, leeks, garlic and pepper. Sprinkle with oil and half the lemon juice, cover, and allow to stand in a cool place for 6 hours.

2 ▲ Heat a large heavy frying pan or skillet. Place the poussins and their marinade in the pan, cover, and cook over moderate heat for about 45 minutes, turning them occasionally. Season with salt during the cooking. Remove to a warm serving platter.

3 ▲ Tilt the pan and spoon off any fat on the surface. Pour in the wine and remaining lemon juice, and cook until the sauce reduces. Strain the sauce, pressing the vegetables to extract all the juices. Place the poussins on individual dishes, and spoon over the sauce. Sprinkle with mint, and serve.

Quail with Grapes

Quaglie con uva

Small birds often feature in Italian recipes. Use the most flavorful white grapes for this dish.

Ingredients
6–8 fresh quail, gutted
salt and freshly ground black pepper
4 tbsp olive oil
¼ cup pancetta or bacon, cut into small dice
1 cup dry white wine
1 cup fresh or canned chicken stock, warmed
12 oz green grapes
serves 4

1 Wash the quail carefully inside and out with cold water. Pat dry with paper towels. Sprinkle salt and pepper into the cavities.

2 Heat the oil in a heavy sauté pan or flameproof casserole large enough to accommodate all the quail in one layer. Add the pancetta or bacon, and cook over low heat for 5 minutes.

3 ▲ Raise the heat to moderate to high, and place the quail in the pan. Brown them evenly on all sides. Pour in the wine, and cook over moderate heat until it reduces by about half. Turn the quail over. Cover the pan, and cook for about 10–15 minutes. Add the stock, turn the quail again, cover, and cook for 15–20 minutes more, or until the birds are tender. Remove to a warmed serving platter and keep warm while the sauce is being finished.

4 ▲ Meanwhile drop the grapes into a pan of boiling water, and blanch for about 3 minutes. Drain and reserve.

5 Strain the pan juices into a small Pyrex cup. If bacon has been used, allow the fat to separate and rise to the top. Spoon off the fat and discard. Pour the strained gravy into a small saucepan. Add the grapes and warm them gently for 2–3 minutes. Spoon around the quail and serve.

Duck with Chestnut Sauce

Petti di anatra con salsa di castagne

This autumnal dish makes use of the sweet chestnuts that are gathered in Italian woods.

Ingredients
1 sprig fresh rosemary
1 clove garlic, thinly sliced
2 tbsp olive oil
4 duck breasts, boned and fat removed
For the sauce
1 lb chestnuts
1 tsp oil
1½ cups milk
1 small onion, finely chopped
1 carrot, finely chopped
1 small bay leaf
salt and freshly ground black pepper
2 tbsp cream, warmed
serves 4–5

1 ▲ Pull the leaves from the sprig of rosemary. Combine them with the garlic and oil in a shallow bowl. Pat the duck breasts dry with paper towels. Brush the duck breasts with the marinade. Allow to stand for at least 2 hours before cooking.

2 Preheat the oven to 350°F. Cut a cross in the flat side of each chestnut with a sharp knife.

~ COOK'S TIP ~

The chestnut sauce may be prepared in advance and kept in the refrigerator for up to 2 days, or it may be made when chestnuts are in season and frozen. Allow to thaw to room temperature before re-heating.

3 ▲ Place the chestnuts in a baking pan with the oil, and shake the pan until the nuts are coated with the oil. Bake for about 20 minutes, then peel.

4 Place the peeled chestnuts in a heavy saucepan with the milk, onion, carrot and bay leaf. Cook slowly for about 10–15 minutes until the chestnuts are very tender. Season with salt and pepper. Discard the bay leaf. Press the mixture through a strainer.

5 Return the sauce to the saucepan. Heat gently while the duck is cooking. Just before serving, stir in the cream. If the sauce is too thick, add a little more cream. Preheat the broiler, or prepare a barbecue.

6 ▲ Broil the duck breasts until medium rare, about 6–8 minutes. The meat should be pink when sliced. Slice into rounds and arrange on warm plates. Serve with the heated sauce.

Roast Pheasant with Juniper Berries

Fagiano arrosto

Sage and juniper are often used in Italian cooking to flavor pheasant and other game.

Ingredients

2½–3 lb pheasant with liver, finely chopped (optional)
3 tbsp olive oil
2 sprigs fresh sage
3 shallots, chopped
1 bay leaf
2 lemon quarters, plus 1 tsp juice
2 tbsp juniper berries, lightly crushed
salt and freshly ground black pepper
4 thin slices pancetta or bacon
6 tbsp dry white wine
1 cup fresh or canned chicken stock, heated
2 tbsp butter, at room temperature
2 tbsp flour
2 tbsp brandy

serves 3–4

1 ▲ Wash the pheasant under cool water. Drain well, and pat dry with paper towels. Rub with 1 tbsp of the olive oil. Place the remaining oil, sage leaves, shallots, and bay leaf in a shallow bowl. Add the lemon juice and juniper berries. Place the pheasant and lemon quarters in the bowl with the marinade, and spoon it over the bird. Allow to stand for several hours in a cool place, turning the pheasant occasionally. Remove the lemon.

2 Preheat the oven to 350°F. Place the pheasant in a roasting pan, reserving the marinade. Sprinkle the cavity with salt and pepper, and place the lemon quarters and bay leaf inside.

3 Arrange some of the sage leaves on the breast of the pheasant, and lay the pancetta or bacon over the top. Secure with string.

4 ▲ Spoon the remaining marinade on top of the pheasant, and roast until tender, about 30 minutes per 1 lb. Baste frequently with the pan juices and with the white wine. Transfer the pheasant to a warmed serving platter, discarding the string and pancetta.

5 Tilt the baking pan and skim off any surface fat. Pour in the stock. Stir over moderate heat, scraping up any meat residues from the bottom of the pan. Add the pheasant liver, if using. Bring to a boil and cook for 2–3 minutes. Strain into a saucepan.

6 ▲ Blend the butter to a paste with the flour. Stir into the gravy a little at a time. Boil for 2–3 minutes, stirring to smooth out any lumps. Remove from the heat, stir in the brandy, and serve.

Veal Escalops with Marsala

Scaloppine di vitello con marsala

This quick and delicious dish enlivens the mild flavor of veal with the sweetness of marsala.

Ingredients

1 lb veal escalops, preferably cut across
    the grain, about ¼ inch thick
½ cup unbleached white flour seasoned
    with salt and freshly ground black
    pepper, for dredging
¼ cup butter
5 tbsp dry marsala wine
5 tbsp stock or water

serves 4

1 Pound the escalops flat to a thickness of about ¼ inch. If they have not been cut across the grain or from one muscle, cut small notches around the edges to prevent them from curling during cooking.

2 ▲ Spread the flour out on a plate. Heat the butter in a large frying pan. Lightly dredge the veal slices in the flour, shaking off any excess. As soon as the foam from the butter subsides, put the veal into the pan in one layer, and brown the slices quickly on both sides, in two batches if necessary. Remove to a warmed serving plate.

3 ▲ Pour in the marsala and the stock. Cook over moderate to high heat for 3–4 minutes, scraping up any meat residues from the bottom of the pan. Pour the sauce over the meat, and serve at once.

Ham and Cheese Veal Escalops

Scaloppine alla bolognese

This dish from Bologna can be made with Parmesan or Gruyère cheese.

Ingredients

8 veal escalops, about 1 lb total,
    preferably cut across the grain
½ cup unbleached white flour seasoned
    with salt and freshly ground black
    pepper, for dredging
2 tbsp butter
2 tbsp olive oil
3 tbsp dry white wine
8 thin slices ham
½ cup freshly grated Parmesan cheese,
    or 8 thin slices Gruyère cheese

serves 4

1 Preheat the oven to 400°F. Pound the escalops flat. If they have not been cut across the grain or from one muscle, cut small notches around the edges to prevent them from curling during cooking. Spread the seasoned flour over a plate.

2 ▲ Heat the butter with the oil in a large frying pan. Lightly dredge the veal slices in the flour, shaking off any excess. As soon as the foam from the butter subsides, put the veal into the pan in one layer, and brown the slices quickly on both sides. Remove to a shallow oven dish. Add the wine to the pan and cook for 1–2 minutes, scraping up the brown residue from the bottom of the pan with a wooden spoon. Pour over the escalops.

3 ▲ Place one slice of ham on top of each escalop. Sprinkle with one tablespoon of Parmesan, or top with one slice of Gruyère. Place in the oven and cook until the cheese melts, 5–7 minutes. Serve hot.

Cold Veal with Tuna Sauce
Vitello tonnato

This classic summer dish is best when prepared in advance and refrigerated for a few hours before serving. The dish can be kept for up to 3 days in the refrigerator.

Ingredients
1¾ lb boneless roasting veal, in
   one piece
1 carrot, peeled
1 stalk celery
1 small onion, peeled and quartered
1 bay leaf
1 clove
1 tsp whole peppercorns
For the tuna sauce
14 oz canned tuna, preferably in olive oil
4 anchovy fillets
2 tsp capers, rinsed and drained
3 tbsp fresh lemon juice
1¼ cups mayonnaise
salt and freshly ground black pepper
capers and pickled cornichons, to garnish
serves 6–8

3 ▲ Scrape the tuna purée into a bowl. Fold in the mayonnaise. Check the seasoning and adjust as necessary.

4 Slice the veal as thinly as possible. Spread a little of the tuna sauce over the bottom of a serving platter.

5 ▲ Arrange a layer of the veal slices on top of the sauce. Cover with a thin layer of sauce. Make another layer or two of veal slices and sauce, ending with the sauce. Garnish with capers and cornichons. Cover with plastic wrap and refrigerate until needed.

1 ▲ Place the veal, vegetables and flavorings in a medium saucepan (not aluminium or copper). Cover with water. Bring to a boil and simmer for 50–60 minutes. Skim off any scum that rises to the surface. Do not overcook, or the veal will fall apart when sliced. Allow it to cool in its cooking liquid for several hours, or overnight.

2 Drain the tuna. Place it in a food processor or blender, and add the anchovies, capers and lemon juice. Process to a creamy paste. If it seems too thick, add 2–3 tbsp of the cool veal stock and process again.

Milanese Stewed Shin of Veal

Ossobuco alla milanese

"Ossobuco" means "hollow bone", and this dish calls for shin of veal cut into sections across the bone. Each bone should have its center of marrow, which is considered a great delicacy.

Ingredients
¼ cup butter
1 clove garlic, peeled and crushed
4 pieces of shin of veal, each about 2 in
 thick
flour, for dredging
salt and freshly ground black pepper
1 cup dry white wine
1¼ cups fresh or canned beef or chicken
 stock
1 bay leaf
1 sprig fresh thyme, or ¼ tsp dried thyme
For the gremolada
1 small clove garlic
2 tbsp chopped fresh parsley
1 tsp chopped lemon zest
½ anchovy fillet (optional)
serves 4

1 Preheat the oven to 325°F. Heat the butter with the crushed garlic clove in a heavy casserole large enough to accommodate all the meat lying flat in one layer. Dredge the veal lightly in the flour. Add it to the pan and brown it first on one side, and then on the other. Season with salt and pepper. Discard the garlic.

2 ▲ Add the wine, and cook over moderate to high heat for 3–4 minutes, turning the veal over several times. Pour in the stock, and add the bay leaf and thyme. Cover the casserole, and place it in the center of the oven. Bake for 2 hours.

3 ▲ In the meantime, prepare the gremolada by combining the garlic, parsley, lemon rind and anchovy, if using, on a board and chopping them together very finely.

4 ▲ After 2 hours, remove the casserole from the oven. Taste the sauce for seasoning. Sprinkle in the gremolada, and mix it well into the sauce. Return the casserole to the oven for 10 more minutes, and serve.

Milanese Veal Chops

Costolette alla milanese

This famous dish depends on the chops being cooked carefully in butter.

Ingredients
2 veal chops or cutlets, on the bone
1 egg
salt and freshly ground black pepper
6–8 tbsp plain breadcrumbs
¼ cup butter
1 tbsp vegetable oil
lemon wedges, to serve
serves 2

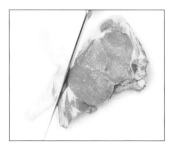

1 ▲ Trim any gristle or thick fat from the chops. Cut along the rib bone, if necessary, to free the meat on one side. Pound the meat slightly to flatten.

2 ▲ Beat the egg in a shallow bowl and season it with salt and pepper. Spread the breadcrumbs over a plate. Dip the chops into the egg, and then into the breadcrumbs. Pat the breadcrumbs to help them to stick.

~ COOK'S TIP ~

Milanese cooks sometimes soak the chops in milk for about an hour to soften the meat.

3 ▲ Heat the butter with the oil in a heavy frying pan large enough to hold both chops side by side. Do not let it brown. Add the chops to the pan, and cook them slowly over low to moderate heat until the breadcrumbs are golden and the meat is cooked through. The timing will depend on the thickness of the chops. The important thing is not to overcook the breadcrumb coating while undercooking the meat. Serve hot with lemon wedges.

Veal Rolls with Sage and Ham

Saltimbocca

These rolls are so good that, as their Italian name implies, they "jump into your mouth".

Ingredients
8 small veal escalops
8 small slices prosciutto
8 leaves fresh sage
salt and freshly ground black pepper
3 tbsp butter
½ cup fresh or canned beef or chicken
    stock, warmed
serves 3–4

1 Gently pound the veal slices with a mallet until thin. Lay a piece of prosciutto over each slice. Top with a sage leaf, and season with salt and pepper. Roll the escalops around the filling and secure each roll with a wooden toothpick.

2 ▲ Heat half the butter in a frying pan just large enough to hold the rolls in one layer. When the butter is bubbling add the veal, turning the rolls to brown them on all sides. Cook for about 7–10 minutes, or until the veal is cooked. Remove to a warmed plate.

3 ▲ Add the remaining butter and the hot stock to the frying pan, and bring to a boil, scraping up the brown residue on the bottom of the pan with a wooden spoon. Pour the sauce over the veal rolls, and serve.

Pizzaiola Steak

Bistecchine alla pizzaiola

This dish comes from Naples, where tomato sauces are used from pizza to meat.

Ingredients
1 lb beef steaks, preferably rump or
    chuck, thinly sliced
3 tbsp flour, for dredging
3 tbsp olive oil
3 cloves garlic, peeled and crushed
1 × 14 oz can plum tomatoes, with their
    juice, passed through a food mill
2 tbsp chopped basil or parsley
salt and freshly ground black pepper
serves 4

1 Trim any excess fat from the steaks, and notch the edges slightly with a sharp knife to prevent them from curling during cooking. Pat the steaks dry with paper towels, and dredge lightly in the flour.

2 ▲ In a large heavy frying pan or skillet, heat 2 tbsp of the oil with the garlic cloves. As soon as they are golden, raise the heat, push them to the side of the pan, and add the steaks. Brown quickly on both sides. Remove the meat to a dish.

3 ▲ Add the tomatoes, the remaining oil, and the herbs to the pan. Season with salt and pepper. Cook over moderate heat for about 15 minutes. Discard the garlic cloves. Return the steaks to the pan, stir to cover them with the sauce, and cook for 4–5 minutes more. Serve.

Herbed Burgers

Polpette

Dress up ground beef with fresh herbs and a tasty tomato sauce.

Ingredients
1½ lb lean ground beef
1 clove garlic, finely chopped
1 scallion, very finely chopped
3 tbsp chopped fresh basil
2 tbsp finely chopped parsley
salt and freshly ground black pepper
3 tbsp butter
For the tomato sauce
3 tbsp olive oil
1 medium onion, finely chopped
11 oz tomatoes, chopped
a few leaves fresh basil
3–4 tbsp water
1 tsp sugar
1 tbsp white wine vinegar
salt and freshly ground black pepper
serves 4

2 Add the water, sugar and vinegar, and cook for 2–3 minutes more. Season with salt and pepper. Remove from the heat, allow to cool slightly, and pass the sauce through a food mill or strainer. Check the seasoning.

3 ▲ Combine the meat with the garlic, scallions and herbs in a mixing bowl. Season with salt and pepper. Form into 4 burgers, patting the meat as lightly as possible.

4 ▲ Heat the butter in a frying pan. When the foam subsides add the burgers, and cook over moderate heat until brown on the underside. Turn the burgers over, and continue cooking until done. Remove to a warmed plate.

5 Tilt the frying pan, and spoon off any surface fat. Pour in the sauce, raise the heat and bring to a boil, scraping up the meat residue from the bottom of the pan. Serve with the burgers.

1 To make the tomato sauce, heat the oil and gently sauté the onion until translucent. Add the tomatoes and cook for 2–3 minutes. Add the basil, cover the pan, and cook for 7–8 minutes over moderate heat.

Meatballs

Polpettine

These meatballs may be eaten as a main course or with pasta or rice. They are also good cold.

Ingredients

2 tbsp dried porcini mushrooms
²/₃ cup warm water
1 lb lean ground beef
2 cloves garlic, finely chopped
4 tbsp chopped fresh parsley
3 tbsp chopped fresh basil
1 egg
6 tbsp plain breadcrumbs
2 tbsp freshly grated Parmesan cheese
salt and freshly ground black pepper
4 tbsp olive oil
1 medium onion, very finely chopped
¼ cup dry white wine
chopped fresh parsley, to garnish
serves 3–4 as a main course

1 Soak the dried mushrooms in the warm water for 15 minutes. Lift them out of the water and chop finely. Filter the soaking water through paper towels and reserve.

2 ▲ In a mixing bowl, combine the meat with the chopped mushrooms, garlic and herbs. Stir in the egg. Add the breadcrumbs and Parmesan, and season with salt and pepper. Form the mixture into small balls 1 ½ inches in diameter.

3 ▲ In a large heavy frying pan or skillet, heat the oil. Add the onion and cook over low heat until soft. Raise the heat and add the meatballs, rolling them often to brown them evenly on all sides. After about 5 minutes add the filtered mushroom soaking water. Cook for 5–8 minutes more, or until the meatballs are cooked through.

4 ▲ Remove the meatballs to a heated serving plate with a slotted spoon or spatula. Add the wine to the pan, and cook for 1–2 minutes, stirring to scrape up any residues on the bottom of the pan. Pour the sauce over the meat balls. Sprinkle with parsley, and serve at once.

Beef Stew with Red Wine   *Spezzatino di manzo con vino rosso*

This rich, hearty dish should be served with mashed potatoes or polenta.

Ingredients

5 tbsp olive oil
2½ lb boneless beef chuck, cut into
    1½ in cubes
1 medium onion, very finely sliced
2 carrots, chopped
3 tbsp finely chopped fresh parsley
1 clove garlic, chopped
1 bay leaf
a few sprigs fresh thyme, or pinch of
    dried thyme leaves
pinch of ground nutmeg
1 cup red wine
1 × 14 oz can plum tomatoes, chopped,
    with their juice
½ cup fresh or canned beef or chicken
    stock
about 15 black olives, pitted and halved
salt and freshly ground black pepper
1 large red sweet pepper, cut into strips
serves 6

1 ▲ Preheat the oven to 350°F. Heat 3 tbsp of the oil in a large, heavy casserole. Brown the meat, a little at a time, turning it to color on all sides. Remove to a side plate while the remaining meat is being browned.

2 When all the meat has been browned and removed, add the remaining oil, the onion and carrots. Cook over low heat until the onion softens. Add the parsley and garlic, and cook for 3–4 minutes more.

3 ▲ Return the meat to the pan, raise the heat, and stir well to mix the vegetables with the meat. Stir in the bay leaf, thyme and nutmeg. Add the wine, bring to a boil and cook, stirring, for 4–5 minutes. Stir in the tomatoes, stock and olives, and mix well. Season with salt and pepper. Cover the casserole, and place in the center of the preheated oven. Bake for 1½ hours.

4 ▲ Remove the casserole from the oven. Stir in the strips of pepper. Return the casserole to the oven and cook, uncovered, for 30 minutes more, or until the beef is tender.

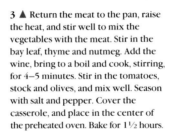

Roast Lamb with Herbs
Arrosto d'agnello con erbe e aglio

This dish originates from southern Italy, where lamb is simply roasted with garlic and herbs.

Ingredients
3 lb leg of lamb
3–4 tbsp olive oil
4 cloves garlic, peeled and cut in half
2 sprigs fresh sage, or pinch of dried sage leaves
2 sprigs fresh rosemary, or 1 tsp dried rosemary leaves
2 bay leaves
2 sprigs fresh thyme, or ½ tsp dried thyme leaves
salt and freshly ground black pepper
¾ cup dry white wine
serves 4–6

1 Cut any excess fat from the lamb. Rub with olive oil. Using a sharp knife, make small cuts just under the skin all around the meat. Insert the garlic pieces in some of the cuts, and a few of the fresh herbs in the others. (If using dried herbs, sprinkle them over the surface of the meat.)

2 Rub the remaining fresh herbs all over the lamb, and allow it to stand in a cool place for at least 2 hours before cooking. Preheat the oven to 375°F.

3 ▲ Place the lamb in a baking pan, surrounded by the herbs. Pour on 2 tbsp of the oil. Season. Place in the oven and roast for 35 minutes, basting occasionally.

4 ▲ Pour the wine over the lamb. Roast for 15 minutes more, or until the meat is cooked. Remove the lamb to a heated serving dish. Tilt the pan, spooning off any fat on the surface. Strain the pan juices into a gravy boat. Slice the meat, and serve with the sauce passed separately.

Lamb Stewed with Tomatoes and Garlic
Spezzatino d'agnello

This rustic stew comes from the plateau of Puglia, where sheep graze alongside vineyards.

Ingredients
2 large cloves garlic
1 sprig fresh rosemary (or 3 tbsp chopped fresh parsley if fresh rosemary is not available)
6 tbsp olive oil
2½ lb stewing lamb, trimmed of fat and gristle and cut into chunks
flour seasoned with freshly ground black pepper, for dredging
¾ cup dry white wine
2 tsp salt
1 lb fresh tomatoes, chopped, or
    1 × 14 oz can tomatoes, chopped
½ cup beef stock, heated
serves 5–6

1 Preheat the oven to 350°F. Chop the garlic with the parsley, if using. Heat 4 tbsp of the oil in a wide casserole.

2 Add the garlic and rosemary or parsley and cook over moderate heat, until the garlic is golden.

3 ▲ Dredge the lamb in the flour. Add the lamb chunks to the pan in one layer, turning to brown them evenly. When brown, remove them to a side plate. Add a little more oil, and brown the remaining lamb.

4 ▲ When all the lamb has been browned, return it to the casserole with the wine. Raise the heat and bring to a boil, scraping up any residues from the bottom. Sprinkle with the salt. Stir in the tomatoes and the stock. Stir well. Cover the casserole, and place in the center of the oven. Bake for 1¾–2 hours, or until the meat is tender.

Pork Braised in Milk with Carrots   *Lonza al latte con carote*

This method of slowly cooking a joint of pork produces a deliciously creamy gravy. It is a speciality of the Veneto region.

Ingredients
1½ lb lean loin of pork
3 tbsp olive oil
2 tbsp butter
1 small onion, finely chopped
1 stalk celery, finely chopped
8 carrots, cut into 2 in strips
2 bay leaves
1 tbsp peppercorns
salt, to taste
2 cups milk, scalded
serves 4–5

1 ▲ Trim any excess fat from the pork, and tie it into a roll with string.

3 ▲ Pour in the hot milk. Cover the casserole and place it in the center of the oven. Bake for about 90 minutes, turning and basting the pork with the sauce about once every 20 minutes. Remove the cover for the last 20 minutes of baking.

4 ▲ Remove the meat from the casserole, and cut off the string. Place the meat on a warmed serving platter and cut into slices.

5 ▲ Discard the bay leaves. Press about one-third of the carrots and all the liquids in the pan through a strainer. Arrange the remaining carrots around the meat.

6 ▲ Place the sauce in a small saucepan, taste for seasoning, and bring to a boil. If it seems too thin, boil it for a few minutes to reduce it slightly. Serve the sliced meat with the carrots, and pass the hot sauce separately.

2 ▲ Preheat the oven to 350°F. Heat the oil and butter in a large casserole. Add the vegetables, and cook over low heat until they soften, 8–10 minutes. Raise the heat, push the vegetables to one side and add the pork, browning it on all sides. Add the bay leaves and peppercorns, and season with salt.

~ VARIATION ~

This dish can also be made using a joint of veal. Substitute a piece of boneless veal and proceed as in the recipe. This dish is delicious served hot or cold.

Pork Fillet with Caper Sauce *Fettine di maiale con salsa di capperi*

The caper sauce can be made in advance and reheated while the pork is sautéed.

Ingredients
1 lb pork fillet, cut into thin slices
flour seasoned with freshly ground black
    pepper, for dredging
2 tbsp butter
2 tbsp olive oil
For the caper sauce
2 tbsp olive oil
¼ cup butter
½ small onion, very finely chopped
1 anchovy fillet, rinsed and chopped
1 tbsp flour
2 tbsp capers, rinsed
1 tbsp finely chopped fresh parsley
4 tbsp wine vinegar
4 tbsp water
4 tbsp balsamic vinegar
serves 4–5

1 Make the sauce by heating the oil and 2 tbsp of the butter in a small saucepan (not aluminum) and slowly cooking the onion. When it is soft, add the anchovy, mashing it into the onion with a wooden spoon.

2 ▲ Stir in the flour and, when it is well amalgamated, the capers and parsley. Add the wine vinegar and water, stirring over low heat to thicken the sauce. Just before serving stir in another 2 tbsp of butter, and the balsamic vinegar.

3 Meanwhile, flatten the pork fillets with a meat pounder until thin. Dredge lightly in the seasoned flour, shaking off any excess.

4 ▲ Heat 2 tbsp of butter and the oil in a large frying pan, and when hot add the pork slices in one layer. Brown the meat on both sides, cooking it for a total of 5–6 minutes. Remove to a heated serving dish, and repeat with the remaining pork slices. Serve hot, with the sauce.

Pork Chops with Mushrooms *Costolette di maiale con funghi*

The addition of dried porcini mushrooms gives fresh cultivated mushrooms a richer flavor.

Ingredients
3 tbsp dried porcini mushrooms, soaked
    in 1 cup warm water and drained
    (reserve the soaking water)
⅓ cup butter
2 cloves garlic, peeled and crushed
11 oz fresh cultivated mushrooms, thinly
    sliced
salt and freshly ground black pepper
1 tbsp olive oil
4 pork chops, trimmed of excess fat
½ tsp fresh thyme leaves, or ¼ tsp dried
    thyme
½ cup dry white wine
⅓ cup light cream
serves 4

1 Filter the mushroom soaking water through a layer of paper towels, and reserve. Melt two-thirds of the butter in a large frying pan. Add the garlic. When the foam subsides, stir in all the mushrooms. Season and cook over moderate heat until the mushrooms give up their liquid, 8–10 minutes.

2 Remove the mushrooms to a side dish. Add the remaining butter and the oil to the frying pan. When hot, add the pork in one layer and sprinkle with thyme. Cook over moderate to high heat for about 3 minutes per side to seal. Reduce the heat, and cook for 15–20 minutes more. Remove to a warmed plate.

3 ▲ Spoon off any fat in the pan. Pour in the wine and the mushroom water. Cook over high heat until reduced by about half, stirring to scrape up the residues at the bottom. Add the mushrooms and the cream, and cook for 4–5 minutes more. Serve the sauce poured over the chops.

Liver with Onions

Fegato alla veneziana

This classic Venetian dish is very good served with grilled polenta. Allow enough time for the onions to cook very slowly, to produce a sweet flavor.

Ingredients
⅓ cup butter
3 tbsp olive oil
1½ lb onions, very finely sliced
salt and freshly ground black pepper
1¾ lb calfs liver, sliced thinly
3 tbsp finely chopped fresh parsley, to
   garnish
grilled polenta wedges, to serve
   (optional)
serves 6

1 ▲ Heat two-thirds of the butter with the oil in a large heavy frying pan. Add the onions, and cook over low heat until soft and tender, about 40–50 minutes, stirring often. Season with salt and pepper. Remove to a side dish.

2 ▲ Heat the remaining butter in the pan over moderate to high heat. When it has stopped bubbling add the liver, and brown it on both sides. Cook for about 5 minutes, or until done. Remove to a warmed side dish.

3 ▲ Return the onions to the pan. Raise the heat slightly, and stir the onions to mix them into the liver cooking juices.

4 ▲ When the onions are hot, turn them out onto a heated serving platter. Arrange the liver on top, and sprinkle with parsley. Serve with grilled polenta wedges, if desired.

Rabbit with Tomatoes

Coniglio con pomodori

Rabbit is very popular in Italy, and is prepared in many ways. This is a hearty dish with strong and robust flavors.

Ingredients
1½ lb boned rabbit, cut into chunks
2 cloves garlic, thinly sliced
½ cup thinly sliced pancetta or lean bacon
1½ lb tomatoes, peeled, seeded and
    roughly chopped
3 tbsp chopped fresh basil
salt and freshly ground black pepper
4 tbsp olive oil
serves 4–5

3 ▲ Place the tomatoes in a layer in the bottom of a baking dish. Arrange the rabbit pieces on top of the tomatoes. Sprinkle with olive oil and place, uncovered, in the oven. Roast for 40–50 minutes.

4 ▲ Baste the rabbit occasionally with any fat in the dish. After the rabbit has cooked for about 25 minutes the dish may be covered with foil for the remaining time if the sauce seems to be too dry.

1 ▲ Preheat the oven to 400°F. Pat the rabbit pieces dry with paper towels. Place a thin slice of garlic on each piece. Wrap a slice of pancetta or bacon around it, making sure the garlic is held in place.

2 ▲ Place the tomatoes in a non-stick pan, and cook them for a few minutes until they give up some of their liquid and begin to dry out. Stir in the basil, and season with salt and pepper.

DESSERTS

This delectable sampler of Italy's most popular family desserts is drawn from many regions and includes scrumptious tarts and creamy puddings, nutty cookies, baked fruits and refreshing summer ices.

Italian Coffee Dessert

Tiramisù

"Tiramisù" means "pick me up", and this rich egg and coffee dessert does just that!

Ingredients
1 lb 2 oz mascarpone cheese
5 eggs, separated, at room temperature
scant ½ cup superfine sugar
pinch of salt
lady fingers or slices of sponge cake, to line dish(es)
½ cup strong Italian espresso coffee
4 tbsp brandy or rum (optional)
unsweetened cocoa powder, to sprinkle
serves 6–8

1 Beat the mascarpone in a small bowl until soft. In a separate bowl beat the egg yolks with the sugar (reserving 1 tbsp) until the mixture is pale yellow and fluffy. Gradually beat in the softened mascarpone.

2 ▲ Using an electric beater or wire whisk, beat the egg whites with the salt until they form stiff peaks. Fold the egg whites into the mascarpone mixture.

3 Line one large or several individual serving dishes with the cookies or cake slices. Add the reserved sugar to the coffee, and stir in the liqueur.

4 ▲ Sprinkle the coffee over the cookies. They should be moist but not saturated. Cover with half of the egg mixture. Make another layer of cookies moistened with coffee, and cover with the remaining egg mixture. Sprinkle with cocoa powder. Refrigerate for at least 1 hour, preferably more, before serving.

Italian Custard

Zabaglione

This airy egg custard fortified with sweet wine is most often eaten warm with cookies or fruit.

Ingredients
3 egg yolks
3 tbsp sugar
5 tbsp marsala or white dessert wine
pinch of grated orange zest
serves 3–4

1 ▲ In the top half of a double boiler, or in a bowl, away from the heat, whisk the egg yolks with the sugar until pale yellow. Beat in the marsala or wine.

2 ▲ Place the pan or bowl over a pan of simmering water, and continue whisking until the custard is a frothy, light mass and evenly coats the back of a spoon, 6–8 minutes. Do not let the upper container touch the hot water, or the zabaglione may curdle.

3 ▲ Stir in the orange zest. Serve immediately.

~ COOK'S TIP ~

A small teaspoon of ground cinnamon may be added to the zabaione.

Italian Trifle

Zuppa inglese

Known in Italy as "English Soup" this is a kind of trifle that has little to do with England!

Ingredients

2 cups milk
grated zest of ½ scrubbed lemon
4 egg yolks
⅓ cup superfine sugar
½ cup flour, sifted
1 tbsp rum or brandy
2 tbsp butter
7 oz lady fingers or 11 oz sponge cake,
    sliced into ½ inch slices
⅓ cup kirsch wasser or cherry brandy
⅓ cup Strega liqueur
3 tbsp apricot jam
fresh whipped cream, to garnish
chopped toasted nuts, to garnish
serves 6–8

1 Heat the milk with the lemon zest in a small saucepan. Remove from the heat as soon as small bubbles form on the surface.

2 ▲ Beat the egg yolks with a wire whisk. Gradually incorporate the sugar, and continue beating until pale yellow. Beat in the flour. Stir in the milk very gradually, pouring it in through a strainer to remove the lemon. When all the milk has been added, pour the mixture into a heavy saucepan. Bring to a boil stirring constantly with a whisk. Simmer for 5–6 minutes, stirring constantly. Remove from the heat and stir in the rum or brandy. Beat in the butter. Allow to cool to room temperature, stirring to prevent a skin from forming.

3 ▲ Brush the cookies or cake slices with the kirsch or cherry brandy on one side, and the Strega liqueur on the other. Spread a thin layer of the custard over the bottom of a serving dish. Line the dish with a layer of cookies or cake slices. Cover with some of the custard. Add another layer of cookies which have been brushed with liqueur.

4 ▲ Heat the jam in a small saucepan with 2 tbsp water. When it is hot, pour or brush it evenly over the cookies. Continue with layers of custard and liqueur-brushed cookies until the ingredients have been used up. End with custard. Cover with plastic wrap or foil, and refrigerate for at least 2–3 hours. To serve, decorate the top of the trifle with whipped cream and garnish with chopped nuts.

Chestnut Pudding

Budino di castagne

Sweet chestnuts are found in the mountainous regions of Italy in October and November.

Ingredients

1 lb fresh sweet chestnuts
1¼ cups milk
½ cup sugar
2 eggs, separated, at room temperature
¼ cup unsweetened cocoa powder
½ tsp pure vanilla extract
⅓ cup confectioners' sugar, sifted
butter, for the mold(s)
fresh whipped cream, to garnish
marrons glacés, to garnish

serves 4–5

1 Cut a cross in the side of the chestnuts, and drop them into a pan of boiling water. Cook for 5–6 minutes. Remove with a slotted spoon, and peel while still warm.

2 ▲ Place the peeled chestnuts in a heavy or non-stick saucepan with the milk and half of the sugar. Cook over low heat, stirring occasionally, until soft. Remove from the heat and allow to cool. Press the contents of the pan through a strainer.

3 Preheat the oven to 350°F. Beat the egg yolks with the remaining sugar until the mixture is pale yellow and fluffy. Beat in the cocoa powder and the vanilla.

4 ▲ In a separate bowl, whisk the egg whites with a wire whisk or electric beater until they form soft peaks. Gradually beat in the sifted confectioners' sugar and continue beating until the mixture forms stiff peaks.

5 ▲ Fold the chestnut and egg yolk mixtures together. Fold in the egg whites. Turn the mixture into one large or several individual buttered pudding molds. Place on a cookie sheet, and bake in the oven for 12–20 minutes, depending on the size. Remove from the oven, and allow to cool for 10 minutes before unmolding. Serve garnished with whipped cream and marrons glacés.

Fruit Salad

A really good fruit salad is always refreshing, and in Italy it comes bathed in fresh orange and lemon juices. Use any mixture of fresh seasonal fruits.

Ingredients
juice of 3 large sweet oranges
juice of 1 lemon
1 banana
1–2 apples
1 ripe pear
2 peaches or nectarines
4–5 apricots or plums
⅔ cup black or green grapes
⅔ cup berries (strawberries, raspberries, etc)
any other fruits in season
sugar, to taste (optional)
2–3 tbsp kirsch, maraschino or other liqueur (optional)
serves 4–6

1 Place the fresh orange and lemon juices in a large serving bowl.

2 ▲ Prepare all the fruits by washing or peeling them as necessary. Cut them into bite-size pieces. Halve the grapes and remove any seeds. Core and slice the apples. Pit and slice soft fruits and leave small berries whole. As soon as each fruit is prepared, put it into the bowl with the juices.

3 ▲ Taste the salad, adding sugar if using. A few tablespoons of liqueur may also be added. Cover the bowl and refrigerate for at least 2 hours. Mix well before serving. In Italy, Fruit Salad is eaten alone, with vanilla ice cream or with zabaglione. It is not usually served with cream.

Baked Apples with Red Wine

Italian baked apples include a delicious filling of sultanas soaked in spiced red wine.

Ingredients
scant ½ cup sultanas
1½ cups red wine
pinch of grated nutmeg
pinch of ground cinnamon
4 tbsp granulated sugar
pinch of grated lemon zest
6 tart apples of even size
3 tbsp butter
serves 6

1 In a small bowl, combine the sultanas with the wine. Stir in the spices, sugar and lemon zest. Allow to stand for 1 hour.

2 Preheat the oven to 375°F. Wash the apples. Use a corer or small, sharp knife to remove the central cores without cutting through to the bottom of the apples.

3 ▲ Divide the sultana mixture between the 6 apples, spooning them into the hollow cores. Spoon in a little extra spiced wine.

4 ▲ Arrange the apples in a buttered baking dish. Pour the remaining wine around the apples. Top each core hole with a knob of butter. Bake for 40–50 minutes, or until the apples are soft but not mushy. Serve hot or at room temperature.

Lemon Ricotta Cake

Torta di limone e ricotta

This lemony cake from Sardinia is quite different from a traditional cheesecake.

Ingredients
6 tbsp butter
¾ cup granulated sugar
generous ⅓ cup ricotta
3 eggs, separated
1½ cups flour
1½ tsp baking powder
grated zest of 1 lemon
3 tbsp fresh lemon juice
confectioners' sugar, for dusting
serves 6–8

1 Grease a 9 inch round cake or springform pan. Line the bottom with parchment paper or waxed paper. Grease the paper. Dust with flour. Set aside. Preheat the oven to 350°F.

2 Cream the butter and sugar together until smooth. Beat in the ricotta.

3 Beat in the egg yolks, one at a time. Add 2 tbsp of the flour, and the lemon zest and juice. Sift the baking powder into the remaining flour and beat into the batter until well blended only.

4 ▲ Beat the egg whites until they form stiff peaks. Fold them carefully into the batter.

5 ▲ Turn the mixture into the prepared pan. Bake for 45 minutes, or until a cake tester inserted in the center of the cake comes out clean. Allow the cake to cool for 10 minutes before turning it out onto a rack to cool. Dust the cake generously with confectioners' sugar before serving.

Peaches with Amaretti Stuffing

Pesche alla piemontese

Peaches are plentiful all over Italy. They are sometimes prepared hot, as in this classic dish.

Ingredients
4 ripe fresh peaches
juice of ½ lemon
⅔ cup crushed amaretti cookies, or 1 cup
    home-made amaretti (see recipe)
2 tbsp marsala, brandy or peach brandy
2 tbsp butter, at room temperature
½ tsp vanilla extract
2 tbsp granulated sugar
1 egg yolk
serves 4

1 Preheat the oven to 350°F. Wash the peaches. Cut them in half and remove the pits. Enlarge the hollow left by the pits by scooping out some of the peach with a small spoon. Sprinkle the peach halves with the lemon juice.

2 ▲ Soften the amaretti crumbs in the marsala or brandy for a few minutes. Beat the butter until soft. Stir in the amaretti mixture and all remaining ingredients.

3 ▲ Arrange the peach halves in a baking dish in one layer hollow side upwards. Divide the amaretti mixture into 8 parts, and fill the hollows, mounding the stuffing up in the center. Bake for 35–40 minutes. These peaches are delicious served hot or cold.

Choux Pastries with Two Custards

Bigné alle due creme

Italian pastry shops are filled with displays of sweetly scented pastries such as these.

Ingredients

scant 1 cup water
½ cup butter
1 in piece vanilla bean
pinch of salt
1¼ cups flour
5 eggs

For the custard fillings

2 oz plain cooking chocolate
1¼ cups milk
4 egg yolks
scant ⅓ cup granulated sugar
generous ⅓ cup flour
1 tsp pure vanilla extract
1¼ cups whipping cream
unsweetened cocoa powder, to garnish
confectioners' sugar, to garnish
makes about 48

1 ▲ Preheat the oven to 375°F. Heat the water with the butter, vanilla and salt. When the butter has melted, beat in the flour. Cook over low heat, stirring constantly, for about 8 minutes. Remove from the heat.

2 ▲ Add the eggs one at a time. Remove the vanilla bean.

3 ▲ Butter a flat cookie sheet. Using a pastry bag fitted with a round nozzle, squeeze the mixture out onto the tray in balls the size of small walnuts, leaving space between the rows. Bake for 20–25 minutes, or until the pastries are golden brown. Remove from the oven and allow to cool before filling.

4 ▲ Meanwhile, prepare the custard fillings. Melt the chocolate in the top half of a double boiler, or in a bowl set over a pan of simmering water. Heat the milk in a small saucepan, taking care not to let it boil.

~ VARIATION ~

The choux pastries may be filled with fresh whipped cream flavored with 1 tsp vanilla or 2–3 tbsp liqueur such as brandy or rum. Spoon the cream into a piping bag and proceed as in Step 6.

5 ▲ Beat the egg yolks with a wire whisk or electric beater. Gradually incorporate the sugar, and continue beating until the mixture is pale yellow. Beat in the flour. Add the hot milk very gradually, pouring it in through a strainer. When all the milk has been added, pour the mixture into a heavy medium saucepan, and bring to a boil. Simmer for 5–6 minutes, stirring constantly. Remove from the heat and divide the custard between two bowls. Add the melted chocolate to one, and stir the vanilla extract into the other. Allow to cool completely.

6 ▲ Whip the cream. Fold half of it carefully into each of the custards. Fill two pastry bags fitted with round nozzles with the custards. Fill half of the choux pastries with the chocolate custard, and the rest with the vanilla custard, making a little hole and piping the filling in through the side of each pastry. Dust the tops of the chocolate-filled pastries with cocoa powder, and the rest with confectioners' sugar. Serve immediately after filling.

Sultana Cornmeal Cookies

Gialletti

These little yellow biscuits come from the Veneto region.

Ingredients
½ cup sultanas
¾ cup finely ground yellow cornmeal
1½ cups plain flour
1½ tsp baking powder
pinch of salt
1 cup butter
1 cup granulated sugar
2 eggs
1 tbsp marsala or 1 tsp vanilla extract
makes about 48

3 Cream the butter and sugar together until light and fluffy. Beat in the eggs, one at a time. Beat in the marsala or vanilla extract.

1 Soak the sultanas in a small bowl of warm water for 15 minutes. Drain. Preheat the oven to 350°F.

2 Sift the cornmeal and flour, the baking powder and the salt together into a bowl.

4 ▲ Add the dry ingredients to the batter, beating until well blended. Stir in the sultanas.

5 ▲ Drop heaped teaspoons of batter onto a greased cookie sheet in rows about 2 in apart. Bake for 7–8 minutes, or until the cookies are golden brown at the edges. Remove to a rack to cool.

Amaretti

Amaretti

If bitter almonds are not available, make up the weight with sweet almonds.

Ingredients
1¼ cups sweet almonds
½ cup bitter almonds
1 cup sugar
2 egg whites
½ tsp almond extract or 1 tsp vanilla extract
confectioners' sugar, for dusting
makes about 36

1 Preheat the oven to 325°F. Peel the almonds by dropping them into a pan of boiling water for 1–2 minutes. Drain. Rub the almonds in a cloth to remove the skins.

2 Place the almonds on a cookie sheet and let them dry out in the oven for 10–15 minutes without browning. Remove from the oven and allow to cool. Turn the oven off.

3 Finely grind the almonds with half of the sugar in a food processor.

4 ▲ Use an electric beater or wire whisk to beat the egg whites until they form soft peaks. Sprinkle half of the remaining sugar over them and continue beating until stiff peaks are formed. Gently fold in the remaining sugar, the vanilla and the almonds.

5 Spoon the almond mixture into a pastry bag with a smooth nozzle. Line a flat cookie sheet with baking parchment paper. Dust this with flour.

6 ▲ Pipe out the mixture in rounds the size of a walnut. Sprinkle lightly with the confectioners' sugar, and allow to stand for 2 hours. Near the end of this time, turn the oven on again and preheat to 350°F.

7 Bake the amaretti for 15 minutes, or until light golden. Remove from the oven and cool on a rack. When completely cool, the cookies may be stored in an airtight container.

Jam Tart

Crostata di marmellata di frutta

Jam tarts are popular in northern Italy, traditionally decorated with pastry strips.

Ingredients

1¾ cups flour
pinch of salt
¼ cup granulated sugar
½ cup butter or margarine, chilled
1 egg
¼ tsp grated lemon zest
1¼ cups fruit jam, such as raspberry,
   apricot or strawberry
1 egg, lightly beaten with 2 tbsp whipping
   cream, for glazing

serves 6–8

1 ▲ Make the pastry by placing the flour, salt and sugar in a mixing bowl. Using a pastry blender or two knives, cut the butter or margarine into the dry ingredients as quickly as possible until the mixture resembles coarse meal. Beat the egg with the lemon zest in a cup, and pour it over the flour mixture. Combine with a fork until the dough holds together. If it is too crumbly, mix in 1–2 tbsp of water.

2 Gather the dough into 2 balls, one slightly larger than the other, and flatten into discs. Wrap in parchment or waxed paper, and refrigerate for at least 40 minutes.

3 Lightly grease a shallow 9 in tart or pie pan, preferably with a removable bottom. Roll out the larger disc of pastry on a lightly floured surface to a thickness of about ⅛ inch.

4 Roll the pastry around the rolling pin and transfer to the prepared pan. Trim the edges evenly with a small knife. Prick the bottom with a fork. Refrigerate for at least 30 minutes.

5 ▲ Preheat the oven to 375°F. Spread the jam evenly over the base of the pastry. Roll out the remaining pastry.

6 ▲ Cut the pastry into strips about ½ inch wide using a ruler as a guide. Arrange them over the jam in a lattice pattern. Trim the edges of the strips even with the edge of the pan, pressing them lightly onto the pastry shell. Brush the pastry with the egg and cream glaze. Bake for about 35 minutes, or until the crust is golden brown. Allow to cool before serving.

Chocolate Nut Tart

Crostata di cioccolata con nocciole

This is a luxurious relative of the simple tart in the previous recipe.

Ingredients
1¾ cups flour
¼ cup granulated sugar
pinch of salt
½ cup butter or margarine, chilled
1 egg
1 tbsp marsala
¼ tsp grated lemon zest
For the filling
1¾ cups dry amaretti cookies, or 2 cups
    home-made amaretti (see recipe)
¾ cup blanched almonds
½ cup blanched hazelnuts
3 tbsp sugar
7 oz plain cooking chocolate
3 tbsp milk
¼ cup butter
3 tbsp liqueur, such as amaretto or brandy
2 tbsp light cream
serves 6–8

1 ▲ Make the pastry as for the Jam Tart, beating the marsala with the egg and lemon zest, and mixing into the dry ingredients.

2 Lightly grease a shallow 9 inch tart or pie pan, preferably with a removable bottom. Roll out the pastry on a lightly floured surface to a thickness of about ⅛ inch. Roll the pastry around the rolling pin and transfer to the prepared pan. Trim the edges evenly with a small knife. Prick the bottom with a fork. Refrigerate for at least 30 minutes.

3 Grind the amaretti to crumbs in a food processor. Remove to a mixing bowl. Set 8 whole almonds aside, and place the rest in the food processor bowl with the hazelnuts and sugar. Grind to a medium texture. Add the nuts to the amaretti, and mix well.

4 ▲ Preheat the oven to 375°F. In the top of a double boiler melt the chocolate with the milk and butter. Stir until smooth.

5 Pour the chocolate mixture into the ground amaretti and nuts, and mix well. Add the liqueur and cream.

6 ▲ Spread the chocolate and nut filling evenly in the pastry shell. Bake for about 35 minutes, or until the crust is golden brown and the filling has puffed up and is beginning to darken. Allow to cool to room temperature. Split the remaining almonds in half, and use them to decorate.

Coffee Granita

Granita di caffè

A granita is a cross between a frozen drink and a flavored ice. The consistency should be slushy, not solid. They can be made at home with the help of a food processor.

Ingredients
2 cups water
½ cup granulated sugar
1 cup very strong espresso coffee, cooled
whipped cream, to garnish (optional)
serves 4–5

1 ▲ Heat the water and sugar together over low heat until the sugar dissolves. Bring to a boil. Remove from the heat and allow to cool.

2 ▲ Combine the coffee with the sugar syrup. Place in a shallow container or freezer tray, and freeze until solid. Plunge the bottom of the frozen container or tray in very hot water for a few seconds. Turn the frozen mixture out, and chop it into large chunks.

3 ▲ Place the mixture in a food processor fitted with metal blades, and process until it forms small crystals. Spoon into serving glasses and top with whipped cream, if desired. If you do not want to serve the granita immediately, pour the processed mixture back into a shallow container or ice tray and freeze until serving time. Allow to thaw for a few minutes before serving, or process again.

Lemon Granita

Granita di limone

Nothing is more refreshing on a hot summer's day than a fresh lemon granita.

Ingredients
2 cups water
½ cup granulated sugar
grated zest of 1 lemon, scrubbed before
   grating
juice of 2 large lemons
serves 4–5

1 Heat the water and sugar together over low heat until the sugar dissolves. Bring to a boil. Remove from the heat, and allow to cool.

2 Combine the lemon zest and juice with the sugar syrup. Place in a shallow container or freezer tray, and freeze until solid.

3 ▲ Plunge the bottom of the frozen container or tray in very hot water for a few seconds. Turn the frozen mixture out, and chop it into large chunks.

4 ▲ Place the mixture in a food processor fitted with metal blades, and process until it forms small crystals. Spoon into serving glasses.

Custard Ice Cream

Gelato di crema

Italian ice creams are soft in consistency, and should not be over-sweet.

Ingredients
3½ cups milk
½ tsp grated lemon zest
6 egg yolks
½ cup granulated sugar
makes about 3¾ cups

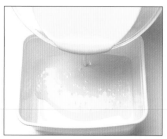

1 Make the custard. Heat the milk with the lemon zest in a small saucepan. Remove from the heat as soon as small bubbles start to form on the surface. Do not let it boil.

2 Beat the egg yolks with a wire whisk or electric beater. Gradually incorporate the sugar, and continue beating for about 5 minutes until the mixture is pale yellow. Strain the milk. Slowly add it to the egg mixture drop by drop.

3 ▲ When all the milk has been added, pour the mixture into the top of a double boiler, or into a bowl placed over a pan of simmering water. Stir over moderate heat until the water in the pan is boiling, and the custard thickens enough to lightly coat the back of a spoon. Remove from the heat and allow to cool.

4 Freeze in an ice cream maker, following the manufacturer's instructions. The gelato is ready when it is firm but still soft.

5 ▲ If you do not have an ice cream maker, pour the mixture into a metal or plastic freezer container and freeze until set, about 3 hours. Remove from the container and chop roughly into 3 in pieces. Place in the bowl of a food processor and process until smooth. Return to the freezer container, and freeze again until firm. Repeat the freezing-chopping process 2 or 3 times, until a smooth consistency is reached.

Chocolate Ice Cream

Gelato al cioccolato

Use good quality plain or cooking chocolate for the best flavor.

Ingredients
3½ cups milk
4 in piece of vanilla bean
8 oz cooking chocolate, melted
4 egg yolks
½ cup granulated sugar
makes about 3¾ cups

1 Make the custard as for Custard Ice Cream, replacing the lemon with the vanilla.

2 Beat the egg yolks with a wire whisk or electric beater. Gradually incorporate the sugar, and continue beating for about 5 minutes until the mixture is pale yellow. Strain the milk. Slowly add it to the egg mixture drop by drop.

3 ▲ Pour the mixture into a double boiler with the melted chocolate. Stir over moderate heat until the water in the pan is boiling, and the custard thickens enough to lightly coat the back of a spoon. Remove from the heat and allow to cool.

4 ▲ Freeze in an ice cream maker, or follow step 5 of Custard Ice Cream, freezing and processing until a smooth consistency has been reached.

Hazelnut Ice Cream

Gelato di nocciola

This popular flavor goes very well with the chocolate and custard ice creams.

Ingredients

½ cup hazelnuts
2 cups milk
4 in piece vanilla bean
4 egg yolks
6 tbsp granulated sugar
serves 4–6

1 Spread the hazelnuts out on a cookie sheet, and place under a broiler for about 5 minutes, shaking the pan frequently to turn the nuts over. Remove from the heat and allow to cool slightly. Place the nuts on a clean dish towel, and rub them with the cloth to remove their dark outer skin. Chop very finely, or grind in a food processor with 2 tbsp sugar.

2 Make the custard. Heat the milk with the vanilla bean in a small saucepan. Remove from the heat as soon as small bubbles start to form on the surface. Do not let it boil.

3 ▲ Beat the egg yolks with a wire whisk or electric beater. Gradually incorporate the sugar, and continue beating for about 5 minutes until the mixture is pale yellow. Add the milk very gradually, pouring it in through a strainer and discarding the vanilla bean. Stir constantly until all the milk has been added.

4 ▲ Pour the mixture into the top of a double boiler, or into a bowl placed over a pan of simmering water. Add the chopped nuts. Stir over moderate heat until the water in the pan is boiling, and the custard thickens enough to lightly coat the back of a spoon. Remove from the heat and allow to cool.

5 ▲ Freeze in an ice cream maker, or follow step 5 of Custard Ice Cream, freezing and processing until a smooth consistency has been reached.

INDEX